Module 11

Writing: A Road to Reading Comprehension

Louisa Moats, Ed.D., and Joan Sedita, M.Ed.

SOPRIS WEST EDUCATIONAL SERVICES
A CAMBIUM LEARNING COMPANY

BOSTON, MA • NEW YORK, NY • LONGMONT, CO

Published and Distributed by

SOPRIS
WEST
EDUCATIONAL SERVICES™

A Cambium Learning™ Company

4093 Specialty Place • Longmont, Colorado 80504
(303) 651-2829 • www.sopriswest.com

191MOD11

Dedication

To Steve, without whom my work would be impossible,
and with whom I have joy in every day.

—LCM

To my husband, Joe—lifelong friend and partner—and to my
mother, Rosalie, who made possible everything I do.

—JS

Acknowledgments

LETRS has been developed with the help of many people. At Sopris West Educational Services, I continue to enjoy the first-class capabilities of Toni Backstrom, LETRS Program Director, and the expertise of the editorial and publishing staff including Lynne Stair, Karen Butler, Tyra Segars, and many others. Michelle LaBorde has contributed extraordinary talent to the design and development of the LETRS CD-ROM. The vision and commitment of Stuart Horsfall, Ray Beck, Chet Foraker, Stevan Kukic, and Steve Mitchell enabled LETRS to have been created.

The national LETRS trainers have helped me to improve LETRS and to deliver the professional development with fidelity. I am most grateful to Carol Tolman, Susan Hall, Anne Cunningham, Marcia Davidson, Marsha Berger, Deb Glaser, Judi Dodson, Anne Whitney, Nancy Hennessy, Mary Dahlgren, Joan Sedita, Linda Farrell, and Susan Smartt for their wisdom, hard work, and companionship in the LETRS endeavor.

Finally, I am grateful to all my colleagues across the country who campaign for the improvement of teacher preparation and professional development.

—LCM

Over the past 30 years, there are many students, teachers, and colleagues who have contributed to the instruction model that is represented in Module 11. In particular, I'd like to thank the faculty and students at Landmark School for enabling me to develop the strategy instruction curriculum, as well as Gail Parker (principal of East Hampton Middle School) and Tim Frazier (principal of Southampton Intermediate School) for enabling me to fine-tune this instruction into an effective, schoolwide model. I would also like to thank Sally Grimes, Sarah Hewitt, Barbara Gardner, and all the fabulous Reading First trainers in Massachusetts whom I have been privileged to work with these past two years.

Finally, a special thanks to Louisa Moats for believing in me and for validating my work by asking me to coauthor LETRS Module 11.

—JS

About the Authors

Louisa C. Moats, Ed.D., is a nationally recognized authority on how children learn to read and why people fail to learn to read. Widely acclaimed as a researcher, speaker, consultant, and teacher, Dr. Moats has developed the landmark professional development program LETRS for teachers and reading specialists.

Between 1997 and 2001, she completed four years as site director for the National Institute of Child Health and Human Development's Early Interventions Project in Washington, D.C., under the direction of Barbara Foorman of the University of Texas. The project included daily work with teachers and children in high-risk, low-performing schools. Dr. Moats spent the previous 15 years as a licensed psychologist and certified school psychologist in private practice in Vermont, evaluating people of all ages and walks of life for academic learning problems.

Dr. Moats began her professional career as a neuropsychology technician before becoming a teacher. She earned her master's degree at Peabody College of Vanderbilt and a doctorate in reading and human development from the Harvard Graduate School of Education. She has been a faculty member at St. Michael's College in Vermont and Simmons College in Boston, and Clinical Associate Professor of Pediatrics at the University of Texas, Houston.

In addition to LETRS, Modules 1–12 (Sopris West Educational Services, 2005, 2006), her authored and coauthored books include:

- *Spelling: Development, Disability, and Instruction* (York Press, 1995)
- *Straight Talk About Reading* (with Susan Hall; Contemporary Books, 1998)
- *Speech to Print: Language Essentials for Teachers* (Brookes Publishing, 2000)
- *Parenting a Struggling Reader* (with Susan Hall; Random House, 2002)

Instructional materials include the Scholastic Spelling program and *Spellography* (Sopris West Educational Services, 2002). Dr. Moats has written numerous journal articles and policy papers, including the American Federation of Teachers' "Teaching Reading *Is* Rocket Science." She continues to focus on the improvement of professional development for teachers through her work with LETRS.

Dr. Moats and her husband divide their time between Idaho and Vermont. Their extended family includes a professional skier, a school psychologist, an alpaca rancher, and an Australian shepherd.

Joan Sedita, M.Ed., is currently founder and director of Sedita Learning Strategies, a consulting and teacher training service in Boxford, Massachusetts. She has worked for 30 years in the education field and has presented reading, writing, and study skills training to thousands of teachers, parents, and related professionals at schools, colleges, clinics, and professional organizations throughout the country.

Joan worked at the Landmark School in Massachusetts for 23 years as a teacher, supervisor, and high school principal. She was also the founder and director of the Landmark College Preparation Program and director of the Landmark Outreach Teacher Training Program. Joan was one of three lead trainers in Massachusetts for the NCLB Reading First Initiative. She is also a national LETRS trainer and an adjunct instructor at Fitchburg State College. Additional experience includes work with Children's Hospital Medical Center, Boston; WGBH/All Kinds of Minds "Developing Minds" video series; Kurzweil Education Group (software development); Lexia Learning Systems; and the Middle School Reading Task Force for the Massachusetts Department of Education. Joan received her BA from Boston College in 1975 and her master's in reading education from Harvard University in 1980.

In addition to coauthoring LETRS Module 11, Joan has authored a number of books and articles, including:

- *Landmark Study Skills Guide* (Landmark Foundation, 1989)
- *Study Skills: A Landmark School Teaching Guide* (2nd edition) (Landmark Outreach Program, 2001)
- STRATEGIES: The Master Notebook Routine (Sedita Learning Strategies, 2002)
- *Active Learning and Study Strategies Using Kurzweil 3000* (Kurzweil Educational Systems, 2003)
- STRATEGIES: The Key Three Routine (Sedita Learning Strategies, 2003)

Contents for Module 11

Overview of LETRS: Language Essentials for Teachers of Reading and Spelling

LETRS is a series of professional development modules for teachers of reading, spelling, and writing—including general and special educators—that:

◆ Teaches in depth the theory and practice of "scientifically based reading instruction."

◆ Fosters insight into *why* specific instructional practices are effective and *how* to implement them.

◆ Engages teachers in a rewarding, informative learning experience.

Content of LETRS Modules Within the Language-Literacy Connection

The content and activities in LETRS help teachers understand:

◆ How students learn to read and write.

◆ The reasons why some children fail to learn.

◆ The instructional strategies best supported by research.

As author of the American Federation of Teachers' "Teaching Reading *Is* Rocket Science" and the Learning First Alliance's "Every Child Reading: A Professional Development Guide"—as well as contributor to the Reading First Leadership Academies—Dr. Moats has used these works and contributions as blueprints for LETRS. The use of LETRS in professional development associated with Reading First and other reading initiatives is now widespread.

The format of LETRS instruction allows for greater depth of learning and reflection than the brief "once-over" treatment these topics are typically given in professional development. Modules are designed for:

◆ Teachers who are in pre-service licensing programs.

◆ Teachers who are implementing a core, comprehensive reading instruction program or an intervention program.

◆ Coaches, mentors, and course instructors who wish to better understand the foundation concepts of effective teaching practices in reading, spelling, and writing.

Users of this material are encouraged to read widely from the list of teacher resources and instructional programs and references in this module, as well as seek out important summary documents, books, and journal articles on reading psychology and research-based reading instruction.

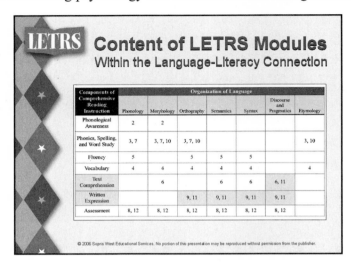

Slide 2

Introduction: Purpose and Goals of the Module

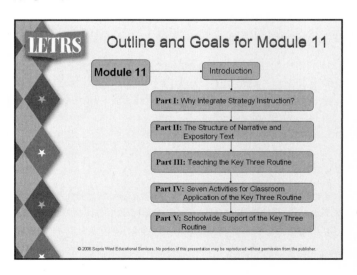

Slide 3

Welcome to LETRS! This module is designed for intermediate, middle school, and high school teachers who wish to learn specific procedures for teaching reading comprehension through skill and strategy instruction that involves written responses. Although there is much more for researchers to learn about enhancement of reading comprehension in the classroom (Kamil, Rosenthal, Pearson, & Barr, 2000; National Reading Panel, 2000; Snow, 2002), researchers agree that comprehension is more likely when students are actively involved in seeking, organizing, and reformulating information in their own words. Written responses demand the mental transformation of ideas and foster ownership of learning (Duke, Pressley, & Hilden, 2004; Hillocks, 1986; Stotsky, 2001). In addition to acquiring a rationale for certain teaching practices, participants in this module will learn several essential strategies that can be employed in any classroom.

Participants who work through this module will:

◆ Review the many causes of reading comprehension difficulties.

◆ Know the research consensus on teaching reading comprehension.

◆ Understand the importance of vocabulary knowledge for comprehension.

◆ Explore text structure and its relationship to comprehension.

◆ Understand and learn to implement the Key Three Routine, a model for comprehension strategy instruction (Sedita, 1989, 2003):

  ● identifying and stating the main idea

  ● taking notes

  ● writing a summary

◆ Understand seven activities that employ the Key Three strategies before, during, and after reading.

◆ Plan schoolwide support for implementation of the Key Three Routine and other study strategies.

The topics covered in this module are represented in the following topic web.

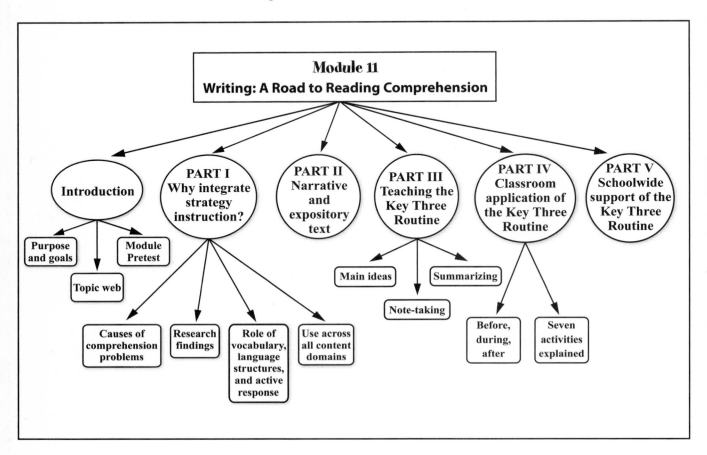

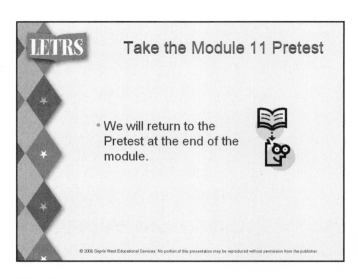

Slide 4

Module 11 Pretest

1. What is the most common underlying cause of reading difficulty in older students (beyond third grade)?

   a. Disinterest in reading.

   b. Dysfluent and inaccurate reading of words in print.

   c. Poverty and its general effects.

   d. Fluent reading without understanding.

2. Which of the following is a reading comprehension instruction strategy that is not on the list of research-supported practices?

   a. Writing a summary.

   b. Using graphic organizers before and after reading.

   c. Clarifying misunderstood ideas as reading is taking place.

   d. Sustained silent reading during school time.

3. One of the most proven and powerful techniques for introducing children to new vocabulary words is:

   a. Embedding each new word in several contextual examples.

   b. Matching definitions to new words before reading.

   c. Asking students to go straight to the dictionary and look up the words.

   d. Concentrating on the most obscure words in the passage.

4. Which of the following statements is **not** true about the relationship among language processing, reading comprehension, and writing?

   a. Taking notes requires awareness of morphology and phrases within sentences.

   b. Stating main ideas requires awareness of the logic of paragraph structure.

   c. Writing a cohesive summary depends in part on the ability to use transition words.

   d. Choosing precise vocabulary words is dependent on rapid automatic naming.

Module 11 Pretest (continued)

5. Narrative and expository text differ in which way?

   a. Expository text is always shorter than narrative text.

   b. Narrative text is usually centered around a problem that the main character(s) must solve; expository text gives factual support for ideas.

   c. Narrative text is more dense and has more Latin-based words than expository text.

   d. Expository text is designed to tell stories, while narrative text is designed to give information about the world.

6. Which of the following statements is true about paragraph main ideas?

   a. Main ideas are often, but not always, found at the beginning of a paragraph.

   b. Main ideas are most often implied and not stated.

   c. In a well-written paragraph, the main idea is stated in the last sentence.

   d. The paragraph main idea is the same as the topic or title.

7. When teachers model comprehension strategies by thinking aloud, they:

   a. Facilitate students' understanding of higher-order comprehension questions.

   b. Show students what good readers do to monitor their understanding.

   c. Help students read narrative and expository texts more accurately.

   d. Not sure

8. A student who has an understanding of story structure:

   a. Will have better oral language skills.

   b. Will be better able to understand and recall expository texts.

   c. Will be better able to understand narrative texts.

   d. Will be better at making speeches.

Module 11 Pretest (continued)

9. To facilitate comprehension, graphic organizers can be used:

    a. Before reading.

    b. After reading.

    c. Before, during, and after reading.

    d. Not sure

10. Main idea webs can be generated from:

    a. Reading stories.

    b. Reading paragraphs.

    c. Reading captions.

    d. Reading textbook chapters.

11. Passage summaries are best generated from:

    a. Key words in the subtitles and illustrations.

    b. Paragraph main ideas.

    c. The ideas that stand out in memory.

    d. The last sentence in each paragraph.

12. What is the most basic step for finding main ideas?

    a. Categorizing

    b. Paragraph level

    c. Multiparagraph level

    d. Not sure

PART I: Why Integrate Comprehension, Study Strategies, and Writing Instruction?

A. Why Do Comprehension Problems Occur?

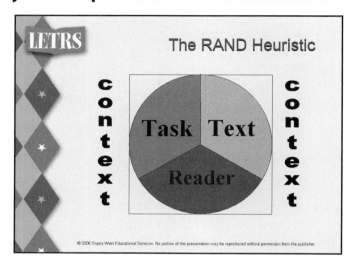

Slide 5

Intermediate, middle school, and high school students' comprehension problems are often attributed to lack of study, motivation, or attention to task. Shouldn't all students be able to learn if they apply themselves to listening and reading carefully? If motivation and effort were indeed the problems, then incentives—such as grades, privileges, and rewards—should be effective remedies for the academic difficulties. Often, however, incentives are not. Lack of motivation to read and lack of sustained attention to the task are often secondary consequences of underlying problems rather than the primary causes of poor reading.

Recent major syntheses of reading comprehension research point out that successful comprehension of written text is influenced by a number of factors, including: (a) the characteristics of the **reader**; (b) the form and nature of the **text** being read; (c) the type and nature of the **reading task** and the **response** that is expected; and (d) the **context** in which the reading takes place (Oakhill & Cain, 1998; Pearson & Gallager, 1983; Peterson, Caverly, Nicholson, O'Neill, & Cusenbary, 2000; Pressley, 2000; Snow, 2002). Each of these dimensions of the reading process may contribute to a successful or unsuccessful **interaction** between the reader and the text.

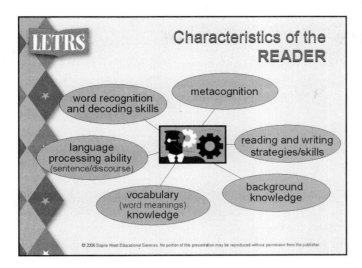

Slide 6

The characteristics of the **reader** include his or her insight, ability to make inferences, and capacity for constructing mental images. The reader brings knowledge of the world, mental models of subject-area content, and a unique set of experiences. The reader also brings a set of learned reading skills that are both linguistic and metacognitive. These include:

◆ the ability to decode the words on the page

◆ knowledge of word and phrase meanings

◆ the ability to read phrases and sentences with sufficient fluency to support comprehension

◆ short-term and working memory capacity to keep ideas on the "cognitive desktop" as meaning is being constructed

◆ the ability to integrate new information into existing mental models (schemata) and extract main ideas

◆ the capacity for emotional response to the text

◆ active searching for connections between what is in the text and what the reader already knows or wants to know.

Whew! No wonder people take different messages from the same text!

[handwritten note: Meta – thinking about what you are thinking about (difficult while rdg)]

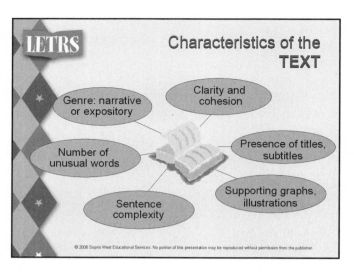

Slide 7

What makes a **text** easier or harder to read? What characteristics of texts affect how they are ranked in difficulty or "leveled"?

Text embodies not only the words we read, but the underlying knowledge structures or mental models (schemata) we must understand to take away the meanings. Further, the words themselves represent idea units in the text base—the thoughts or meanings that each word, phrase, and sentence represent. The degree to which the surface representation (the language) conveys the underlying ideas and their relationship to one another (the propositions) has much to do with whether the text is understandable.

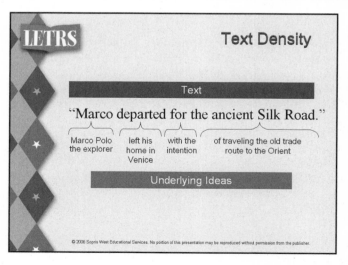

Slide 8

Texts vary by genre: a **narrative** tells a story, an **expository** text explains or gives factual information. Other genres such as letters, poetry, and dramatic dialogues also have distinctive forms and conventions. Texts vary in their proposition density; textbooks usually contain a high number of new ideas or propositions per sentence, while narratives may have a lower

concentration of new or distinct ideas and thus can be easier to understand. Texts may vary in the number of unfamiliar or unusual words, the length of the sentences, the connectedness of those sentences, and the figures of speech used to express ideas. Some texts are "reader-friendly" because they are clearly organized, complete, explicit, and visually easy to scan, while others are more difficult to navigate. For example, a text with an introduction, subtitles, illustrations, and repetition of main ideas in summary passages or lists is easier to manage than one in which those text organizers are lacking. All of these factors may influence how well the reader comprehends the meaning of the text.

"Sometimes I wonder if English really is my native tongue."

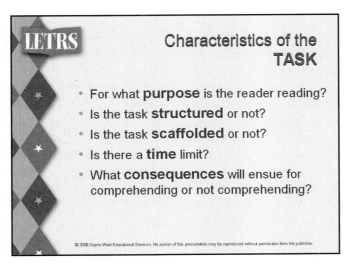

Characteristics of the TASK

- For what **purpose** is the reader reading?
- Is the task **structured** or not?
- Is the task **scaffolded** or not?
- Is there a **time** limit?
- What **consequences** will ensue for comprehending or not comprehending?

Slide 9

The **task** is what the reader is supposed to do or intends to do with the text. Is the text to be read superficially or deeply? Is the text supposed to supply information, to amuse, or to direct? Is the reading task imposed or selected? All of these circumstances may affect motivation to persist with reading for meaning. Reading for a specific purpose may also be linked with a specific consequence. Extrinsically imposed consequences for reading may include test scores, grades, or products that will be

[handwritten notes in right margin: "structure hard tasks", "consistent structure eg. graphic organizer"]

judged by others. Intrinsic consequences include satisfaction, frustration, enlightenment, amusement, or access to information necessary for some ancillary purpose. The purpose or motivation with which one reads can affect many aspects of reading itself. The purpose of the reading can affect the strategies selected during and after reading as well as the pace of reading. If a task is viewed as unimportant, irrelevant, or impossible to understand, then reading is likely to be superficial and comprehension is likely to suffer.

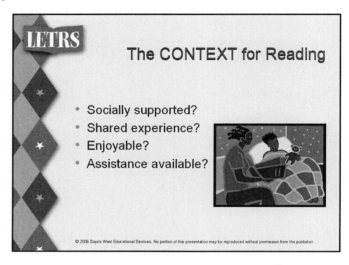

Slide 10

Finally, the **context** in which reading occurs affects comprehension. How much assistance is available if something is not understood? Is the reading a social experience or an individual experience? Are there time constraints? Can ideas be shared with others for whom understanding is important? In a supportive context, students are more likely to persist with challenging material and to grapple with challenges to their understanding. Support can be emotional or cognitive. "Scaffolding" is the process of modeling and encouraging strategic, successful reading by providing structure, organization, questioning, clarification, summarizing, or tying information to what is known or what will be found out (Roehler & Cantlon, 1997). Peer partners, parents, small groups, teacher leaders, or computers can provide instructional scaffolding.

The many ways that comprehension can be interfered with are more apparent when we look at the process from all these angles. Complex problems with multiple, interacting causes usually require multifaceted solutions. Facilitating comprehension may involve improving the readers' skills, selecting or adapting text, changing the expectations or nature of the assignment, or fostering a context in which successful independent reading can occur (Harvey & Goudvis, 2000; Pressley, Brown, El-Dinary, & Afflerbach, 1995).

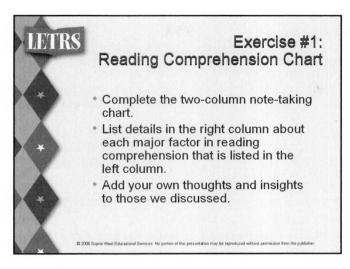

Slide 11

- Key strategy
  selection

At just strategy

- text
- requirements

Exercise #1: Reading Comprehension Chart

- ◆ Major factors that affect reading comprehension are listed in the left column.

- ◆ List details in the right column, beginning with some of the factors mentioned in the section we've just covered.

- ◆ Then, feel free to add your own insights into the impact of each of these factors.

Major Factors in Reading Comprehension	Details: Dimensions of Each Factor
Reader/Writer	
Text	

Major Factors in Reading Comprehension	Details: Dimensions of Each Factor
Task	
Context	

B. Research Support for Effective Comprehension Instruction

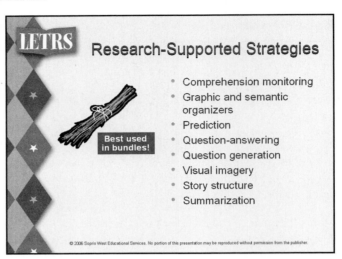

Slide 12

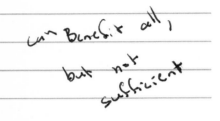

can Benefit all, but not sufficient

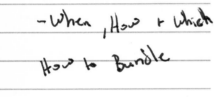

–When, How + Which

How to Bundle

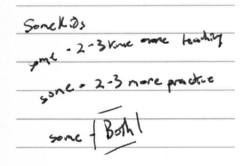

Some Kids
some – 2-3 time more teaching
some – 2-3 more practice
some + Both!

Visual Imagery needs to be paired w/ another (young Kids prediction)

Several recent reviews and syntheses of research provide critical guidance about reading comprehension instruction (Carlisle & Rice, 2002; Kamil et al., 2000; National Reading Panel, 2000; Snow, 2002; Stone, Silliman, Ehren, & Apel, 2004). Referring to hundreds of scientific and quasi-scientific studies, these leading experts generally agree that comprehension can be enhanced by teaching a relatively small set of comprehension strategies. The skills and strategies taught are the skills and strategies typically used by good readers, and they include:

◆ **Comprehension monitoring.** Readers learn to react if they do not understand, rather than passively "skipping" or abandoning material that has not been understood. They approach a text with a sense of purpose and adjust how they read to suit that purpose. They clarify misunderstandings as they read (Klingner & Vaughn, 1999; Lenz & Bulgren, 1995; Texas Center for Reading and Language Arts, 2002).

◆ **Use of graphic and semantic organizers (including story maps).** Readers create or complete graphic or spatial representations of the topics and main ideas in a text, showing how those topics or ideas are related to one another (Dickson, Simmons, & Kame'enui, 1995).

◆ **Prediction.** After previewing a text or reading a portion of the text, the reader predicts what the text will be about or what will happen next in a narrative. The reader seeks to confirm or contradict those predictions (Brody, 2001).

◆ **Question-answering.** Readers answer questions posed by the teacher or by peers and receive immediate feedback on their response. They know whether the answer to a question is located in the text or if the answer must be inferred (Beck, McKeown, Hamilton, & Kucan, 1997).

◆ **Question-generation.** Readers ask questions of themselves or their peer group before, during, and after reading. They learn to consider what type of question is being asked according to a framework (such as Bloom's Taxonomy) and to anticipate test questions they may be asked (Anderson & Krathwhohl, 2001).

◆ **Visual imagery.** Students create mental images of settings, characters, objects, and ideas mentioned in the text (Gambrell & Bales, 1986).

◆ **Story structure.** Students use the structure of the story as a means of helping to predict or recall story content in order to retell, summarize, or answer questions about what they have read (Pressley et al., 1995).

◆ **Summarization.** Readers select the main ideas of expository text and integrate those ideas into a brief paragraph or several paragraphs that capture the most important propositions or ideas in the reading (Duke et al., 2004).

Furthermore, research has shown that although each of these strategies is helpful when used alone, instruction is even more effective when several strategies are combined or used together in a flexible, responsive interaction between the teacher and the students (Duke et al., 2004; Gaskins, 1998; Pressley, 2000).

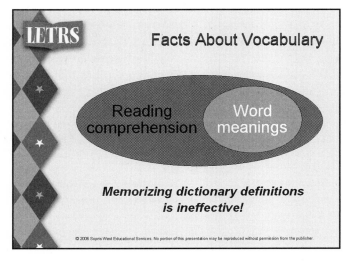

Slide 13

C. Vocabulary: An Essential Knowledge Base for Comprehension

Knowledge of word meanings is a major contributor to text comprehension. The National Reading Panel (2000) confirmed that the depth and breadth of a learner's vocabulary contributes substantially to proficient reading. Understanding a written passage requires knowledge of the individual words that carry the unique meanings in that text. Vocabulary is so important to verbal reasoning ability that psychologists and researchers use it as a proxy for verbal intelligence. Consequently, explicit and implicit exploration of word meanings should occur often during reading instruction, and teachers should choose words deliberately for instruction to make the best use of instructional time.

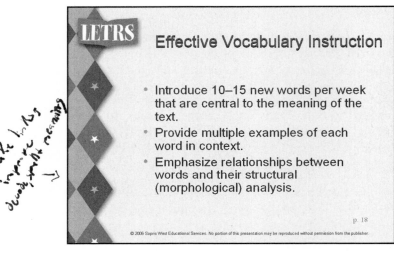

can make links improve vocabulary meaning

Slide 14

Looking up dictionary definitions is most ineffective

if do, ① words they know
② + have some knowledge of

should check on retention →

purpose
'cause time consuming

One of the findings of research in comprehension is that telling students to look up a list of unfamiliar words in a dictionary and memorizing definitions is one of the most *ineffective* approaches to instruction (Stahl, 1999; Stahl and Fairbanks, 1986). What can replace that common practice? Several of the points we emphasized in Module 4 of LETRS, which we will revisit here, include:

- ◆ Select 10–15 new words per week for in-depth study.

- ◆ Choose words to teach that are central to the meaning of the text and that are essential for understanding a content area, not just one selection.

- ◆ Use the words orally in classroom dialogue; provide many contextualized examples of a word's use, and encourage students to use the words in classroom conversation and writing.

- ◆ Provide a conceptual organization within which a word's meaning might be understood; teach words in relation to other words.

◆ Teach the relationship between word structure, word origin, and word meaning (e.g., prefixes, roots, suffixes).

Children who are learning English (ELL) or who have limited language development will require intensive, deliberate instruction in word meanings in addition to phonics and word recognition. Children learning English may be more adept at decoding than they are at interpreting what they read. The size of the child's vocabulary in his or her first language will affect how readily he or she learns the vocabulary of a second language. Word-learning in the first language and overall language proficiency in ELL children is related to the ease with which they learn English.

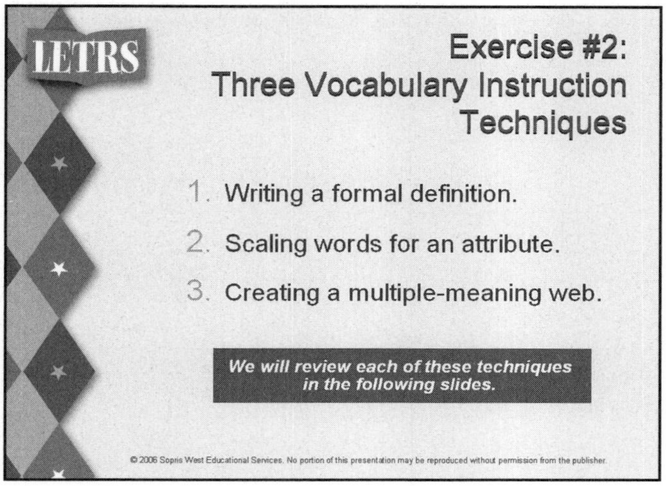

LETRS

Exercise #2:
Three Vocabulary Instruction
Techniques

1. Writing a formal definition.

2. Scaling words for an attribute.

3. Creating a multiple-meaning web.

We will review each of these techniques
in the following slides.

© 2006 Sopris West Educational Services. No portion of this presentation may be reproduced without permission from the publisher.

Slide 15

Exercise #2: Three Vocabulary Instruction Techniques

1. **Writing a formal definition.** A formal or classical definition has two parts: Part A names the category to which something belongs or gives a synonym for the word; Part B gives some critical attributes of the concept.

Example: **Allegiance** is:

A. loyalty

B. usually to a social organization, a set of governing principles or a symbol of those principles

Write a definition for the word **alien** (i.e., citizenship status). _____

_____

_____

_____

Write a definition for the term **isosceles triangle**. _____

_____

_____

Write a definition for the word **ion**._____

_____

2. **Scaling words for an attribute.** Construct a scale or continuum showing the relationship of these words to one another:

**disturbance, apocalypse, debacle, catastrophe, disaster,
calamity, upheaval, misfortune, ruin**

_____

_____

_____

Exercise #2: Three Vocabulary Instruction Techniques (continued)

3. **Creating a multiple-meaning web.** Make a web for multiple meanings of the word **right**. In each box, write a phrase that exemplifies the word's use as well as a brief definition of that particular meaning of **right**.

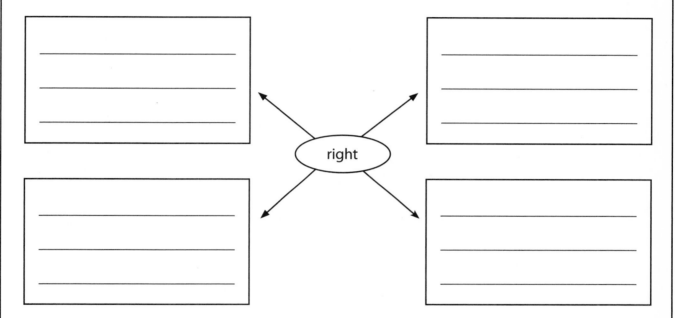

Language Structure	Role in Comprehension	Role in Writing
Punctuation		
Transition words		
Sentence structure		
Paragraph structure		
Essay structure		
Text markers		
Expository text		
Story structure		
Graphic organizers		

Language: The Common Denominator

© 2006 Sopris West Educational Services. No portion of this presentation may be reproduced without permission from the publisher.

Slide 16

D. Language Structure: Links Among Comprehension, Study Strategies, and Writing

Language processing is the common denominator of reading and writing. Researchers have documented for 25 years the causal relationship between oral language proficiency and written language processing. Although phonological processing, or awareness of the speech sounds of a language, has been shown repeatedly to determine how well students of all ages can read words, other language factors come into play in comprehension. Knowledge of vocabulary, ability to interpret phrases and figurative language, understanding of sentence structure, anticipation of paragraph logic and discourse organization—all these factors contribute to both reading comprehension and writing (Berninger & Richards, 2002; Carlisle & Rice, 2002). For example:

♦ Spelling requires knowledge of phonemes, graphemes, orthographic patterns, high-frequency words, and word meanings.

♦ Taking notes requires knowledge of morphology and key phrases for abbreviated notations.

♦ Finding and stating main ideas requires knowledge of sentence and paragraph structures as well as precise vocabulary.

♦ Creating graphic organizers/outlines requires knowledge of text structures to organize and visually represent information.

♦ Summarizing requires knowledge of sentence and discourse structures, proper use of transition words to write summaries, recognition of the propositional structure in narrative or expository text, and the ability to select main points.

Effective instruction stimulates and develops many language skills within the reading/writing lesson, often in parallel (Moats, 2004).

Writing: A Road to Reading Comprehension

Table 11.1. The Comprehension-Writing Connection: Using Language Structures to Gain or Convey Meaning

This chart identifies the language structure that must be processed during reading comprehension and writing.

Reading comprehension and writing are two symbolically mediated and complementary aspects of language use. Language structure is processed to gain (comprehend) or convey (write) intended meanings. Reading comprehension entails input processing (decoding); writing entails output processing (encoding).

Language Structure	Role in Reading Comprehension	Role in Writing
Rules of capitalization and punctuation in orthography	Assist the reader in identifying proper nouns and the beginning and ending of sentences. Provide information about phrasing and emphasis.	Enable the writer to offer clues to the audience about sentence structure, phrasing, and emphasis.
Transition or connecting words	Serve as signals to the reader to anticipate the text structure and the relationships between or among ideas in sentences and paragraphs.	Enable the writer to present ideas in a more organized format, to link ideas in the text, and to tell the audience the structure of the ideas.
Sentence structure (syntax and the rules of grammar)	The reader uses knowledge of syntax to chunk parts of sentences into meaningful units, to confirm recognition of words, and to infer the meaning of unfamiliar words.	The writer uses knowledge of syntax to vary sentence structure, to create compound and complex sentences, and to make the writing richer through the use of advanced parts of speech.
Paragraph structure	The reader uses paragraph structure to identify main ideas (stated or implied) and supporting details.	The writer uses paragraph structure to organize writing into main idea chunks and to convey that structure by indenting each new paragraph.
Essay structure	Helps the reader identify the theme and conclusion while reading as well as the main points that support the theme.	Helps the writer to present a clear statement of theme and to organize ideas into a structure that supports the development of the theme.
Expository text markers (headings, subheadings, and other visual clues)	Provide clues and a framework for chunking reading into manageable units; help the reader identify the hierarchy of main ideas and subordinate ideas.	The writer can use headings and subheadings to organize ideas during writing and to provide the audience with a guide for identifying the hierarchy of ideas.

Language Structure	Role in Reading Comprehension	Role in Writing
Expository text patterns (cause and effect, comparison/contrast, enumeration, etc.)	Help the reader determine a pattern by which the information is presented in the text and how details are related.	Enable the writer to relate details in a way that indicates the relationship of those details.
Narrative story structures	The reader uses story structures to identify the characters, setting, sequence of events, and plot/theme.	The writer uses story structures to clearly convey information about the characters, setting, sequence of events, and plot/theme of the story. The writer also uses story structure to let the audience know the type of narrative (e.g., folktale, biography, short story).
Graphic organizers, outlines	Help the reader to organize and process the information in the reading material and to remember what has been read.	Help the writer to organize story ideas before writing, to develop a plan for the writing, and to follow the plan during writing.

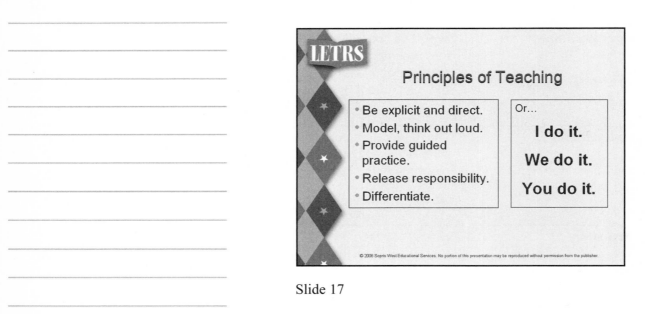

Slide 17

E. Active Response and Other Principles of Teaching and Learning

Written responses demand active involvement in learning. Active involvement in learning, in turn, helps minimize the adverse impact of attention, memory, and executive function problems in intermediate, middle school, and high school students. Successful programs for older, poor readers—beyond early elementary school—apply combinations of strategies that often involve written responses (Barton & Heidema, 2002; California Department of Education, 2000; Curtis & Longo, 1999; Grossen, 2004; Lovett & Steinbach, 1997; Meltzer, Smith, & Clark, 2002; Meltzer & Montague, 2001; Moats, 2004; Pisha & O'Neill, 2003; Rashotte, MacPhee, & Torgesen, 2001; Stotsky, 2001; Swanson, Hoskyn, & Lee, 1999). Written responses require the careful choice of words and academic language structures that are expected in school and workplace settings.

The following instructional practices result in better student outcomes than nondirective, incidental, or implicit methods:

◆ **Be explicit and direct**—Teachers explain the concepts and strategies instead of hoping that students will discover them.

◆ **Model the thought processes**—Teachers talk about why and when certain strategies are applied, demonstrate meta-comprehension by "thinking aloud," and apply the thought processes to several examples.

◆ **Provide guided practice**—Teachers plan activities that enable students to practice with support and obtain corrective feedback.

◆ **Employ a "gradual release of responsibility" model**—Students gradually take over the strategy and apply it independently.

◆ **Differentiate instruction**—Teachers provide adjustments according to student characteristics and assessment data.

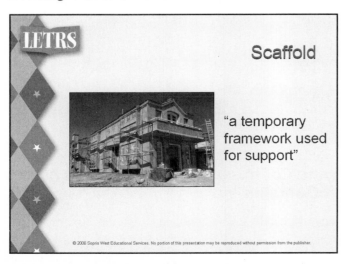

The concept of **"scaffolding"** is important in differentiating instruction. Scaffolding provides additional structure and prompting for students in the forms of:

◆ offering explanations

◆ inviting student participation

◆ verifying and clarifying student understanding

◆ modeling desired behaviors

◆ inviting students to contribute clues for reasoning through a strategy.

Struggling readers in particular need explicit instruction by content-area teachers to transfer reading strategies to a variety of texts. Research indicates that scaffolding must take place across the curriculum and that reading strategies not supported by content teachers have little chance of being transferred by struggling secondary readers. Strategies must be reinforced across the curriculum over a period of years (Gaskins, 1998).

Thus, the teacher's role in comprehension instruction is to not only question or test students after they have read a selection, but also to help students interact with the text. Teachers foster understanding by showing and prompting students to use the thinking skills of a good reader before, during, and after reading.º

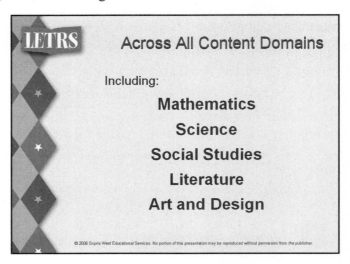

Slide 19

F. Applying Comprehension Instruction Across All Content Domains

Strategies can be used for narrative and expository reading in a variety of subject areas—including mathematics. Strategies are most effective when they are simple to implement in content classrooms. Students will need structure and support while practicing skills for whatever length of time necessary to incorporate them into their working habits, but if all classrooms use the techniques, habits will be consolidated more quickly.

Much of the strategy instruction can (and should) take place in regular-content classrooms with the texts normally used in the class. Classroom teachers can differentiate the instruction and materials for struggling students and provide support for a longer period of time. Strategy instruction in any extra support tutorial should be consistent with what is taught in content classes, and content materials (i.e., textbooks, handouts) from those classes should be used to practice strategies even though students may be receiving special instruction.

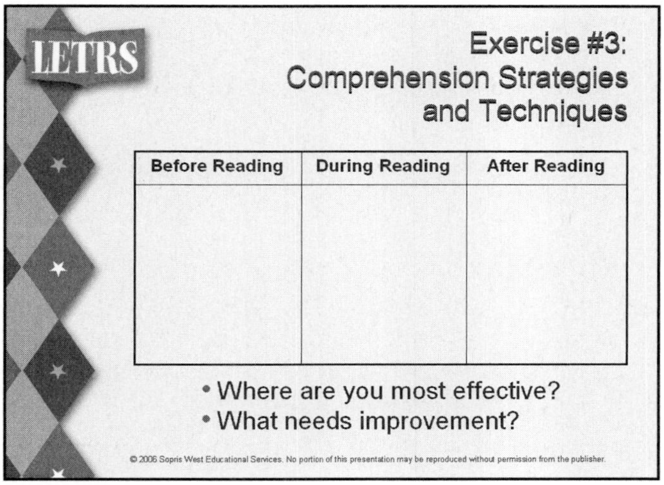

LETRS

Exercise #3:
Comprehension Strategies
and Techniques

Before Reading	During Reading	After Reading

• Where are you most effective?
• What needs improvement?

© 2006 Sopris West Educational Services. No portion of this presentation may be reproduced without permission from the publisher.

Slide 20

During probably toughest/ sparsest, but most important for many struggling kids.

Exercise #3: Comprehension Strategies and Techniques

◆ List the strategies and techniques you now routinely use to teach comprehension.

Before Reading	During Reading	After Reading

◆ Circle the domain(s) in which you feel you are most effective.

◆ Share with a colleague something you feel is working well to foster comprehension in your classroom as well as something that you feel needs improvement.

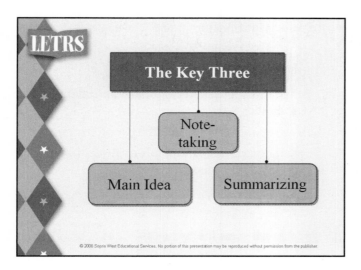

Slide 21

G. Why Emphasize the Key Three Routine?

This module highlights and incorporates the Key Three Routine, a model for comprehension strategy instruction (Sedita, 1989, 2003). This model stresses the skills of identifying and stating the main idea; note-taking; and writing a summary. These three skills form the basis for seven activities that address the comprehension strategies supported by research. Any one of the activities can be used, but students will experience greater organization and long-term memory of the information if they apply at least three or four of the activities. Basic skills, such as discerning main ideas, should be tackled first because they form the foundation for more advanced skills, such as note-taking and summarizing. Moreover, if the strategies are applied across all content-area classes, student learning is likely to be internalized and generalized.

The Key Three strategies accomplish the following instructional goals:

◆ Before reading:
  ● To build and/or to activate students' prior knowledge of the topic.
  ● To put the topic into a "big picture" or context.
  ● To begin reading with a plan to organize information gained from the text.

◆ During reading:
  ● To read with reflection and purpose.
  ● To distinguish main ideas from details and relevant from irrelevant information.
  ● To interpret the language (words, sentences) in which a text is written.

  ● To restate information in one's own words.

◆ After reading:

  ● To return to and elaborate "the big picture," in relation to both the ideas in the text and the connections between the text and other texts or experiences.

  ● To transfer information into long-term memory.

  ● To practice expressing that information in written language appropriate to an academic setting.

PART II: The Structure of Narrative and Expository Text

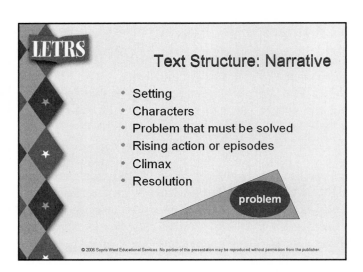

Slide 22

Well-written text follows an organizational structure that facilitates the reader's comprehension. It is organized into paragraphs, chapters, or a larger discourse structure that follows conventions of genre or type of text. **Narrative** text structure usually has a setting, characters who include the protagonist or main character, a problem that the main character is trying to solve, episodes or segments of action that lead toward a problem solution, a climax or reckoning that resolves the problem, and a conclusion that ties up loose ends. Plots are typically arranged around themes, such as man against himself, man against man, or man against nature. Narrative text may be realistic, biographical, or fictional.

Writing: A Road to Reading Comprehension

Story Recipe: Idea Generator

Characters
Who? Traits?

- Three little pigs - 2 carefree; 1 worker
- Big Bad Wolf - hungry, big eater

Setting
Where? When?

- In the country
- Once upon a time

Plot
What happened?

Beginning event: The three pigs each built a house.

Nature of problem: The wolf was hungry. The pigs had built two weak houses and one strong house.

Character's action: The wolf chased the pigs into their houses. It wanted to eat them.

What happened: The wolf huffed and puffed and blew the first two weak houses down. The pigs ran for safety to the third house, which the wolf did not blow down.

Consequence
Result at end? Meaning?

The pigs were safe at the end because of a strong house.
The moral: take time, plan, do the job well.

LETRS

Text Structure: Expository

- Nonfiction
- Explains ideas or information
  (e.g., **ex-** = "out"; **pos** = "to put").
- Has a logical structure.
- Often contains new vocabulary
  (e.g., Latin or Greek derivatives).
- Has more new ideas per
  paragraph than fiction.

Slide 23

Expository text is nonfiction. Expository text usually explains information, provides a sequential or descriptive report, presents evidence or argument, or makes comparisons among ideas. Also called *informational text*, exposition often includes headings and subheadings, illustrations and diagrams that depict ideas, and a format that includes an overview and a summary. Expository text is overwhelmingly more prevalent in academic reading than narrative text, as text-based instruction in social studies, history, science, and math is accomplished with exposition. Expository text can also be distinguished from other literary genres and text structures, including poetry, drama, journalistic reporting, and rhetoric or speech-making.

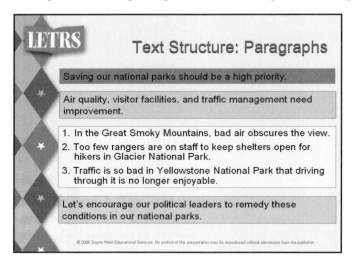

Slide 24

Paragraph structure is especially relevant to the comprehension of expository text. A paragraph is much more than a series of sentences that begin with an indentation. It is about a single topic or idea; it is a cluster of sentences that explicate one main thought. The key idea resides in the topic sentence if the paragraph is well-formed. The key idea is elaborated with supporting details that are often followed by a restatement or concluding sentence.

In all grades, children can benefit from several kinds of practice with these text structures so that they develop familiarity with the underlying organization of ideas in text and improve their ability to extract a main idea.[1] Children can identify the topic sentence in a well-formed paragraph, write or select a topic sentence for a paragraph, rearrange sentences to make paragraphs, find sentences that do not fit into a given paragraph structure, and identify the logical structure of the information with the help of a graphic organizer. Color-coding sentences by their function is a good way to illustrate the job each sentence in a paragraph does (dark blue highlighted sentence: the topic; green highlighted sentence: an elaboration/extension of the topic; yellow highlighted sentences: additional details to support the topic; light blue highlighted sentence: a restatement of the topic or a concluding thought):

Dyslexia is a learning disorder characterized by difficulty with written language. The word **dyslexia** comes from Greek, with the prefix **dys-** meaning "poor" or "inadequate," and the root **lexis** meaning "words" or "language." Many people think that

---

[1] An excellent tool for this type of work with children is Joanne Carlisle's *Reading and Reasoning* (1982). Color-coding is used throughout Auman's *Step Up to Writing* program (2002).

dyslexia means seeing things backward or making reversals, but that is not the case. Nor is it true that boys are more likely to be dyslexic than girls. Far from a rare disorder, dyslexia affects up to 15% of the population. Dyslexia is a common problem that all educators should be able to recognize.

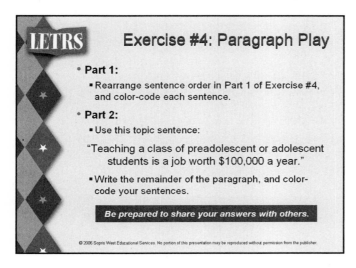

Slide 25

Exercise #4: Paragraph Play

Part 1:

◆ Given these sentences, which one(s) should be dark blue? Green? Yellow? Light blue?

◆ Rearrange the sentence order according to the color-coded sentence hierarchy.

Fortunately, brain science also shows that the dyslexic brain can be "normalized" in response to appropriate teaching.

Connections between sounds, symbols, and meanings are hard to establish.

The dyslexic brain overrelies on the front part of the language (left) hemisphere and is slow to activate posterior regions, which are responsible for fast word recognition.

Dyslexia results from differences in the structure and function of the brain.

For example, before remediation is successful, the brains of dyslexic students may try to read by relying on the right cerebral hemisphere rather than the left.

Several brain areas are activated in support of normal reading, but the dyslexic brain does not exhibit normal activation patterns on fMRI.

Part 2:

◆ Given this topic sentence, write the rest of the paragraph. "Teaching a class of preadolescent or adolescent students is a job worth $100,000 a year."

◆ Highlight or notate your sentences dark blue, green, yellow, and light blue.

_____

_____

_____

_____

_____

_____

_____

_____

_____

_____

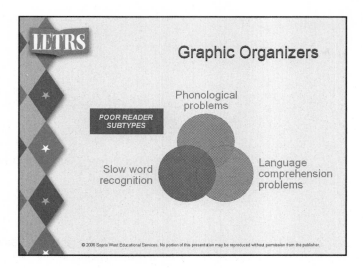

Slide 26

Paragraph and overall text structure can be represented with graphic organizers. A graphic organizer is a visual representation of the logical relationships among ideas. Graphic organizers help many students understand how ideas are connected, especially those with good nonverbal, visual-spatial abilities. Some students, however, may have difficulty comprehending an abstract visual representation of information structure. Graphic organizers can be used to assist students in summarizing what they have read, in preparing to read about a new topic, and in preparing to write an informational piece.

Examples of Graphic Organizers That Depict Discourse Structure

Attribute Wheel

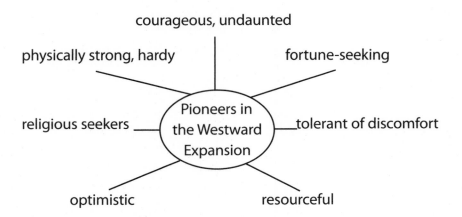

Class Example Map

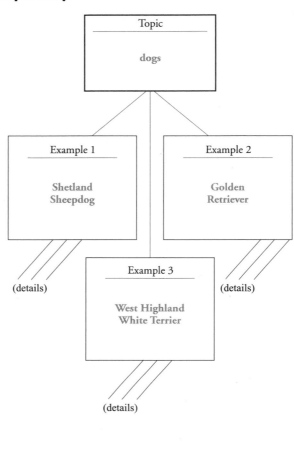

Process (Time Sequence) Map

Goal:	Write a research report
1st	Choose a topic
2nd (Next)	Conduct research
3rd (Next)	Create an outline
Last; finally	Write your paper
Result:	A well-constructed report

Reason (Explanation) Map

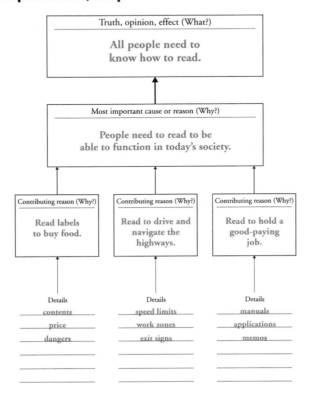

Compare-Contrast Paragraph or Essay

	Idea 1		Idea 2
State	Golden Retrievers make good pets.	(What?)	Shetland Sheepdogs make good pets.

	Similarities (both what?)
Compare	- dogs - long hair - working class - long noses - feathered tails

	Differences (1 is _____ but 2 is _____)
Contrast	- GR larger than SSD (appearance) - GR one color / SSD multicolor (appearance) - GR calm / SSD skittish (personality) - GR bred to retrieve / SSD bred to herd (work)

	Significance (Why important?)
Conclude	It is important to know the similarities and differences between dogs to select the best pet for your family.

Slide 27

There are many sources for prepared graphic organizers. An Internet search for the topic "graphic organizers" yields hundreds of Web sites that offer free downloads of graphic organizers. Inspiration® and Kidspiration® (www.inspiration.com/home.cfm) are two software programs that can be used by teachers and students to create and print graphic organizers.

PART III: Teaching the Key Three Routine

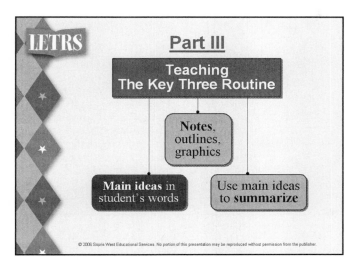

Slide 28

A. What Are the Key Three Skills?

The Key Three Routine highlights three basic comprehension, writing, and study skills. They are:

♦ Identification and formulation of **main ideas** in the student's own words.

♦ Organization and writing of critical information in **notes**, **outlines**, or **graphic organizers**.

♦ Use of the main ideas as a basis for creating an oral or written **summary**.

These three skills are incorporated into seven activities that are applied to a variety of subject-area reading, classroom assignments, and homework. Teacher support and classroom practice are provided, using existing content curriculum and materials. The desired outcome of instruction is independent student application of the strategies in the study of literature, social studies, science, and math.

The Key Three Routine is useful because it helps students to process information at both literal and inferential levels, to identify and organize key points about a topic, and to place that information in long-term memory to be retrieved when it is needed. Active learning strategies—particularly those that involve a written response—prevent students from passively "reading through" material. Although some students intuit and develop these strategies on their own, most need direct instruction to learn

the strategies and require supervised practice before they can apply them independently.

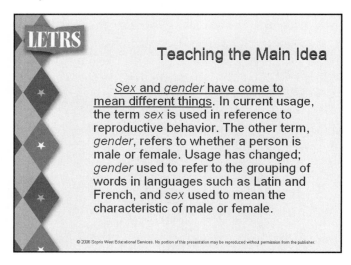

Slide 29

B. How to Teach Identifying and Stating the Main Idea

The ability to recognize and write out main ideas in one's own words is the most important comprehension, writing, and study skill. Comprehending a textbook, getting information from class discussions and lecture, organizing thoughts before writing, and studying for tests all require identification of main ideas and recognition of the details that support them. It is impossible to write a well-structured paragraph on a test or report, or to outline a chapter for studying, unless one can identify the main ideas.

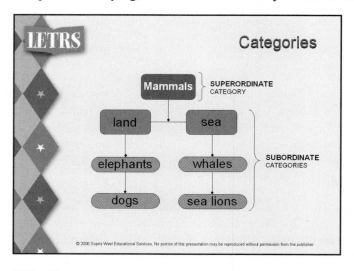

Slide 30

Writing: A Road to Reading Comprehension

From categorizing to multilevel main ideas.

Grouping items or information by category is a natural way of organizing; examples in everyday life surround us. Department stores display goods according to common categories such as men's clothing, women's shoes, kitchenware, and so forth. Food, dishes, and cooking utensils are stored in kitchen cabinets and drawers by category. Clothes in a dresser drawer are organized by function (e.g., shirts in one drawer, underwear and socks in another) so that they can be easily retrieved. The daily newspaper organizes articles in sections such as city news, arts and leisure, and sports. Nonfiction books in the library are identified and stored by category using classification systems such as the Dewey decimal system for subjects such as history, travel, and biology.

Identifying main ideas is sometimes described as "chunking," "getting the gist," identifying the topic or theme, or "seeing the forest through the trees." Some students automatically recognize patterns of organization based on grouping and have a natural tendency to organize their school materials, papers, and information by main ideas. Other students do not intuit this skill, especially in its application to comprehending reading or class lessons. They need direct instruction to see how this concept can be applied to schoolwork.

"Here's to missing the big picture."

Two Kinds of Main Ideas

- Can be:
  1. a **topic** main idea:
     Mammals
  2. a **statement** main idea:
     *Mammals have five defining
     characteristics that distinguish
     them from other vertebrates.*

© 2006 Sopris West Educational Services. No portion of this presentation may be reproduced without permission from the publisher.

Slide 31

What is a main idea?

A main idea can be the category for a list of words, the topic sentence of a paragraph, the theme of an essay or lecture, or the subject of a textbook chapter. There can be several levels of main ideas. For example, a reading selection might have one major main idea for the whole selection, a few section main ideas, and a number of paragraph main ideas. A textbook chapter might include a single chapter subject, major main ideas for each section of the chapter, subject main ideas that correlate with the boldface headings, and paragraph main ideas that support the headings.

A topic is not the same as a main idea statement. A topic is the general subject of a paragraph, multiparagraph selection, or chapter, and can usually be stated in one or two words. A main idea statement is more specific and tells what is being said about the topic. In the slide example above, the topic is "Mammals," and the main idea is "Mammals have five defining characteristics that distinguish them from other vertebrates."

- ◆ A **topic main idea** identifies the category or domain of information that the discourse is about (types of mammals).

- ◆ A **statement main idea** summarizes the salient proposition, or unifying idea, in the discussion of that topic (mammals have five defining characteristics).

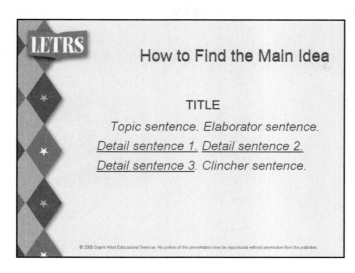

Slide 32

A process for finding the main idea.

The process for determining a main idea is the same whether a student is categorizing a list of words, identifying the main idea of a paragraph, or identifying levels of main ideas in a chapter. That process includes these three steps:

1. Identify the details.

2. Compare the details to determine what they have in common.

3. Use your own words to paraphrase what they have in common.

When a list of words is categorized, the words are the details. They are compared and a common category is identified, which becomes the main idea. For example, "family members" or "relatives" are main ideas for the words **wife**, **brother**, **father**, **niece**, **grandmother**.

Notice that the main idea is always extracted by comparing details and looking for common conceptual threads. In most paragraphs, the main idea is embedded as a topic sentence, although some paragraph main ideas are implied and must be inferred by the reader. When the sentences in a paragraph are compared for common ideas, a main idea can be extracted. For a section in a textbook, the paragraphs are the details that are compared to determine the section main idea. Likewise, the section main ideas are the details that are compared to determine the topic main idea of the chapter.

The examples on page 45 include a paragraph with a stated main idea in a topic sentence, and a paragraph for which the main idea must be inferred by the reader.

Slide 33

Type 1 Example: Paragraph with a stated main idea

(Social studies, expository text)

In the movies, the life of a pirate seems adventurous and exciting. In reality, however, it was difficult and dangerous. The pirates did not eat well because fresh food rotted quickly. They ate mostly hardtack (a dry, plain biscuit) and dried meat, which didn't give them much nutrition. Water often went bad, forcing the pirates to drink beer and rum instead. Many pirates got food poisoning or seasickness. The ships had no toilets and smelled terribly.[2]

Main Idea: Pirate life was difficult and dangerous.

Topic Sentence: Second sentence

Type 2 Example: Paragraph with an unstated or implied main idea

(Science, expository text)

Light passes through the epidermis to reach inner cells known collectively as *mesophyll*. The cells of the mesophyll are where almost all photosynthesis takes place. The shape and arrangement of the upper cells maximize the amount of photosynthesis that takes place. The many air spaces between the cells of the lower layer allow carbon dioxide, oxygen, and water vapor to flow freely.[3]

Main Idea: The internal structure of a leaf promotes photosynthesis (no topic sentence).

---

[2]Archer, A., Gleason, M., & Vachon, V. (2004). *REWARDS Plus: Application to social studies* (Teacher's Guide, pp. 74–75). Longmont, CO: Sopris West Educational Services. Used with permission of the authors and publisher.

[3]Maton, A., & Hopkins, J. (1997). *Exploring life science* (2nd ed.), p. 232. Upper Saddle River, NJ: Pearson Prentice Hall. Used with permission of the publisher.

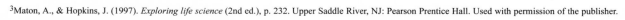

Exercise #5:
Is the Main Idea Stated or Implied?

• Read Paragraph 1 ("Black Elk Speaks")
  or Paragraph 2 ("Marco Polo").

• Determine the main idea in the reading.

• Write the topic sentence, if there is one.
  If there is no topic sentence, create one.

© 2006 Sopris West Educational Services. No portion of this presentation may be reproduced without permission from the publisher.

Slide 34

Exercise #5: Is the Main Idea Stated or Implied?

◆ Read the following two paragraphs.

◆ Identify the main idea in each paragraph.

◆ Indicate where the topic sentence is located in each paragraph. If there is no topic sentence, write one of your own.

Paragraph 1:

There was a war game that we little boys played after a big hunt. We went out a little way from the village and built some grass tepees, playing we were enemies and this was our village. We had an advisor, and when it got dark he would order us to go and steal some dried meat from the big people. He would hold a stick up to us and we had to bite off a piece of it. If we bit a big piece, we had to get a big piece of meat, and if we bit a little piece, we did not have to get so much. Then we started for the big people's village, crawling on our bellies, and when we got back without getting caught, we would have a big feast and a dance and make kill talks, telling of our brave deeds like warriors. Once, I remember, I had no brave deed to tell. I crawled up to a leaning tree beside a tepee and there was meat hanging on the limbs. I wanted a tongue I saw up there in the moonlight, so I climbed up. But just as I was about to reach it, the man in the tepee yelled "Ye-a-a!" He was saying this to his dog, who was stealing some meat too, but I thought the man had seen me, and I was so scared I fell out of the tree and ran away crying.[4]

Main Idea:

_____

_____

Topic Sentence:

_____

_____

[4]Black Elk. (2000). *Black Elk speaks: Being the life story of a holy man of the Oglala Sioux (as told through John J. Neihardt)*, p. 45. Lincoln, NE: University of Nebraska Press.

Paragraph 2:

Born in Italy in the middle of the 13th century, Marco Polo was part of a wealthy merchant family. His father and uncle had already been trading extensively with Middle Eastern countries. They traded silk, porcelain, and other exotic goods over the Silk Road. The Silk Road was a trading route established between China and Rome. As a result, the Polos traveled a great deal. Marco did not meet his father until he was 15 or 16, when his father returned to Venice after many years of travel. This time, when he left again, he took young Marco with him.[5]

Main Idea:

_____

_____

_____

Topic Sentence:

_____

_____

LETRS Sequence for Teaching
the Main Idea (MI)

1. Categorize, find, or write the MI for a list.
2. In single-paragraph readings:
   • Identify the explicitly stated MI.
   • Write MI's that are implied (not stated) in one's own words.
3. In multiparagraph readings:
   • Identify the topic MI and supporting statement MI's.
4. In longer chapter readings:
   • Identify topic MI's.
5. Practice in a variety of subject areas.

© 2006 Sopris West Educational Services. No portion of this presentation may be reproduced without permission from the publisher.

Slide 35

Teaching main idea skills.

Teaching should begin with examples of paragraphs that have a clear topic sentence and supporting details. Even though paragraphs in typical texts often do not contain good paragraph structures, instruction should start

[5]Archer, A., Gleason, M., & Vachon, V. (2004). *REWARDS Plus: Application to social studies* (Teacher's Guide, pp. 62–63). Longmont, CO: Sopris West Educational Services. Used with permission of the authors and publisher.

with model paragraphs that are developed around a single main idea and that use sentences related to that topic. A quick review of many middle school and high school textbooks will reveal paragraphs that contain more than one main idea, a single main idea spread over several paragraphs, and paragraphs that consist of only a single detail sentence. (It may appear as if the textbook writers indented every once in a while for visual relief rather than for the expression of a logical structure!) After students are adept at dealing with logically structured paragraphs, they can be taught how to identify and organize main ideas from less-structured text. The first, structured examples, however, should come from or be about the material already being used in class.

Main idea skills begin with simple categorizing and become increasingly more complex as the reading becomes longer. The following scope and sequence should be followed for introducing main idea instruction:

1. Categorize and find the main idea for a list of words.

2. Identify main ideas from paragraphs with topic sentences.

3. Infer and formulate main ideas from paragraphs without a topic sentence.

4. Identify the topic main idea and supporting paragraph main ideas from a multiparagraph selection.

5. Identify chapter, section, topic, and paragraph main ideas from lengthier selections.

6. Practice main idea skills with both narrative and expository text from a variety of subject areas (e.g., history, science, language arts, math).

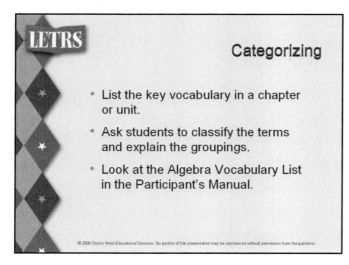

Slide 36

Suggestions for categorizing.

The content-specific vocabulary that is taught in most content classes provides a good opportunity for categorizing. Categorizing a list of new vocabulary will promote learning of the words and provide practice in finding a main idea. The teacher can suggest the categories, or students can be asked to determine their own categories as part of the assignment. The following example is from a ninth-grade unit about the language used in algebra.

Algebra Vocabulary List	
base	The variable *x* in an expression
conclusion	The part of a conditional statement following the word **then**
conditional statement	Statements written in the form of: *If A, then B*
coordinate	The number that corresponds to a point on a number line
counterexample	A specific case in which a statement is false
deductive reasoning	The process of using rules, definition, facts, or properties to reach a valid conclusion
equation	A mathematical sentence that contains an equals sign (=)
evaluate	To find the value of an expression
factor	The quantity being multiplied in an algebraic equation
graph	To draw or plot the points named by certain numbers or ordered pairs on a number line or coordinate plane
hypothesis	The part of a conditional statement immediately following the word **if**
if-then statements	Conditional statements in the form of: *If A, then B*
inequality	An open sentence that contains the symbol $<$, $\leq$, $>$, or $\geq$
negative number	Any value less than zero
open sentence	A mathematical statement with one or more variables
positive number	Any value greater than zero
product	The result of quantities being multiplied in an algebraic expression
solution	A replacement value for the variable in an open sentence
variables	Symbols used to represent unspecified numbers or values
x coordinate	The first number in an ordered pair
y coordinate	The second number in an ordered pair

Options for categories:

Mathematical expressions and solving equations: open sentence, solution, equation, inequality, base, variables, evaluate, factor, product

Vocabulary associated with logical reasoning: conclusion, conditional statement, if-then statements, hypothesis, deductive reasoning, counter-example

Graphing numbers: positive number, negative number, graph, coordinate, x coordinate, y coordinate

One-syllable or two-syllable words: base, factor, graph, product

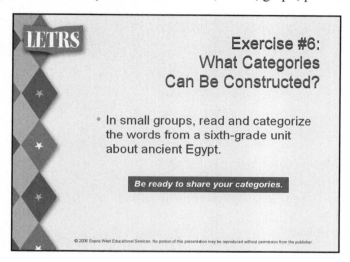

Slide 37

Exercise #6: What Categories Can Be Constructed?

◆ Create categories for these vocabulary words from a sixth-grade unit about ancient Egypt.

amulet: a charm worn to bring good luck

Anubis: the god of embalming and guide for the newly dead

Book of the Dead: a collection of spells/prayers to help with the passage to the afterlife

canopic jars: containers for the internal organs of an embalmed body

cartouche: an oval shape surrounding an inscription of a royal name

cataracts: steep rapids in a river

Delta: the point at which water leaves a river and enters the sea

Giza: the place where the pyramids were built

Hatshepsut: the first female ruler of the New Kingdom of Egypt

Imhoptep: the architect who designed the first pyramid for King Zoser

inundation: the annual flooding of the Nile

Kush: a country to the south of Egypt

Luxor: the place of royal cemeteries

mastaba: a rectangular-shaped tomb with sloping sides and a flat top

Menes: the king who first unified upper and lower Egypt

natron: a mineral/salt used in mummification

obelisk: a tall and thin four-sided stone pillar

papyrus: a water reed that was used for making paper

Pharaoh: the title for the rulers of Egypt

Ra: the first and most important Egyptian god

Red Sea: the sea that borders Egypt on the east

sarcophagus: a stone coffin

Exercise #6: What Categories Can Be Constructed? (continued)

scarab: an amulet in the form of a beetle

scribes: professional writers or recordkeepers

shroud: a cloth in which a dead body is wrapped

sphinx: a statue with the head of a human and the body of a lion

tributary: a small river that feeds into the Nile

Possible categories:

_____

_____

_____

_____

_____

_____

_____

_____

_____

_____

_____

_____

_____

_____

_____

_____

_____

_____

_____

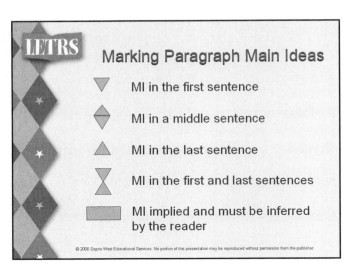

Slide 38

Suggestions for paragraph main ideas.

A paragraph is the most basic unit of discourse, consisting of several sentences that support one main idea. A key factor in successful reading comprehension is the ability to identify paragraph main ideas, and then combine and compare those ideas to determine the general theme and concepts in the reading. If students cannot identify paragraph main ideas, their reading comprehension will suffer.

When students initially learn to write paragraphs, they usually include a topic sentence at the beginning of the paragraph. However, they must be taught that the topic sentence can also appear in the middle or at the end of a paragraph. McWhorter (1983) developed a series of visual symbols that help students visualize where a topic sentence is positioned:

▽ In the first sentence

◇ In a middle sentence

△ In the last sentence

⧖ In the first and last sentences (i.e., topic sentence and con-cluding sentence)

Some paragraphs do not include a topic sentence; the main idea must be inferred by comparing the detail sentences. Identifying and stating inferred main ideas is more difficult for students, especially those with weak language-expression skills. Key words can be "borrowed" from a topic sentence, while the wording for an inferred main idea must be generated completely by the student. The following symbol can be used to indicate that there is no stated main idea and that it must be inferred:

☐ Implied main idea that must be inferred

Placing these symbols in the margin next to the paragraphs in a reading selection can help students identify where the topic sentence is located in each paragraph. Another option for helping students identify the main ideas is to underline the topic sentences in paragraphs. If the main idea must be inferred, the student will see there is no sentence underlined.

If paragraphs in a reading selection are not structured, teachers can also provide guidelines in the margins by using arrows, brackets, and numbers to help identify main ideas. The example on the next two pages combines all three methods.

Example: *Topic sentence symbols, underlined main ideas, and use of brackets to help structure multiparagraph reading*

What Is a Mammal?[6]

 <u>About 200 million years ago, the first mammals appeared on Earth.</u> They evolved from a now-extinct group of reptiles. The first mammals were very small and looked something like the modern-day tree shrew.

 Today there are about 4000 different kinds of mammals living on Earth. In addition to humans and sea otters, mammals include whales, bats, elephants, duckbill platypuses, lions, dogs, kangaroos, and monkeys. Because scientists group together animals with similar characteristics, you might wonder <u>what such different-looking animals have in common.</u>

 Mammals have characteristics that set them apart from all other living things. Mammals <u>are warm-blooded vertebrates that have hair or fur and that feed their young with milk produced in mammary glands.</u> In fact, the word **mammal** comes from the term *mammary gland*. Another special characteristic of mammals is that they provide their young with more care and protection than do other animals.

 At one time during their lives, <u>all mammals possess fur or hair.</u> If it is thick enough, the fur or hair acts as insulation and enables mammals such as musk oxen to survive in very cold parts of the world. Musk oxen are the furriest animals alive today. Indeed, the fur of an adult musk ox may be as deep as 15 centimeters! Mammals can also survive in harsh climates because <u>they are warm-blooded.</u> Recall from Chapter 12 that warm-blooded animals maintain their body temperatures internally as a result of the chemical reactions that occur within their cells. Thus, mammals maintain a constant body temperature despite the temperature of their surroundings. What other group of animals can do this?

<u>The circulatory system of mammals consists of a four-chambered heart and an assortment of blood vessels.</u> The heart pumps oxygen-poor blood to the lungs, where the blood exchanges its carbon dioxide for oxygen. After leaving the lungs, the oxygen-rich blood returns to the heart and is pumped to all parts of the body through blood vessels.

[6] Maton, A., & Hopkins, J. (1997). *Exploring life science* (2nd ed.), pp. 365–367. Upper Saddle River, NJ: Pearson Prentice Hall. Used with permission of the publisher.

Mammals have the most highly developed excretory system of all the vertebrates. Paired kidneys filter nitrogen-containing wastes from the blood in the form of a substance called *urea* (yoo-REE-uh). Urea combines with water and other wastes to form urine. From the kidneys, urine travels to a urinary bladder, where it is stored until it passes out of the body.

 The nervous system of mammals consists of a brain that is the most highly developed of all the animals. The brain makes thinking, learning, and understanding possible; coordinates movement; and regulates body functions. Mammals also have highly developed senses that provide them with information about their environment. For example, humans, monkeys, gorillas, and chimpanzees are able to see objects in color. This characteristic is extremely useful because these mammals are most active during the day when their surroundings are bathed in light. Many animals—cats, dogs, bats, elephants, for example—are more sensitive to certain sounds than humans are.

 Like reptiles and birds, all mammals have internal fertilization, and males and females are separate individuals. However, the way in which mammals reproduce differs. The differences in reproduction provide a means of classifying mammals into three main groups. These groups are egg-laying mammals, pouched mammals, and placental (pluh-SEHN-tuhl) mammals. Egg-laying mammals, as their name implies, lay eggs. Pouched mammals give birth to young that are not well-developed. Thus, the young must spend time in a pouch-like structure in their mother's body. In placental mammals, the young remain inside the mother until their body systems are able to maintain life on their own. At birth, these young are more developed than are those who spend time in their mother's pouch. You will learn more about each group of mammals in the remainder of this chapter.

Exercise #7: Delineating and Coding Main Ideas

- First, study the coded example, "What Is a Mammal?", on pages 56–57 of the Participant's Manual.
- Then, read the "Viruses" article in the exercise.
- Place symbols in the left margin to show where the paragraph main ideas are located.

We will check our answers on an overhead.

© 2006 Sopris West Educational Services. No portion of this presentation may be reproduced without permission from the publisher.

Slide 39

Writing: A Road to Reading Comprehension

Exercise #7: Delineating and Coding Main Ideas

◆ Read this article.

◆ Underline the topic sentences, and place symbols in the margin to identify the location and type of main ideas. Watch for paragraphs that should be divided into two because two main ideas are included. Use brackets to divide these paragraphs.

Viruses[7]

Have you ever had a cold or the flu? The coughing and sneezing, aches and fevers are all the work of a tiny virus living inside some of your body's cells. How can such a tiny thing cause you to feel so awful?

All living things, like plants and animals, share common behaviors that include growing, developing, reproducing, and responding to surroundings. Things that do not share these behaviors are nonliving things such as air, metal, and sand. Perched between the boundary of living and nonliving things are viruses, which are tiny, infectious particles that are considered by some scientists to be living things and by others to be nonliving things. If viruses are floating around in the air or sitting on a kitchen counter, they are inert, having as much life as a rock. However, unlike nonliving things, viruses can live and reproduce. When they attach to a suitable plant, animal, or bacterial cell, referred to as a host cell, they infect and take over the cell. To live and to reproduce, they must invade a host cell and use it.

Viruses are not cells, even though they have some substances also found in cells. Viruses are particles that are about a thousand times smaller than bacteria. These tiny particles contain genetic instructions that give the virus its characteristics, such as shape and how to reproduce. Viruses are wrapped in a protein coat. Some types of viruses also have a membrane around the protein.

Viruses are around you all the time. They enter your body through your mouth or nose or through breaks in your skin. Different types of viruses require different types of host cells. The protein coat on the virus helps it detect the right kind of host cell. For example, a virus that causes a respiratory infection would detect and attack cells that line the lungs.

Once the host cell is detected, the virus attaches itself to the outside of the cell (*adsorption*). It then injects its genetic information through the cell membrane and into the host cell (*entry*). The host cell's enzymes obey the virus's genetic instructions, creating new virus particles (*replication and assembly*). New particles leave the host cell in search of other host cells, where the cycle then

---

[7] Archer, A., Gleason, M., & Vachon, V. (2004). *REWARDS Plus: Reading strategies applied to science passages* (Teacher's Guide, pp. 167–169). Longmont, CO: Sopris West Educational Services. Used with permission of the authors and publisher.

Exercise #7 (continued)

continues (*release*). The host cell may be destroyed during this process. As the virus spreads, you begin to feel more and more sick. Carefully examine the flowchart below to better understand how viruses work.

In order to look at a virus, you would have to look through an electron microscope. Electron microscopes are much more powerful than those you use at school, which may only be able to see bacteria. Remember that viruses are many times smaller than most bacteria cells. Scientists use electron microscopes to see the tiniest of particles.

Different kinds of viruses have different shapes. Some viruses are polyhedral, meaning that they have many sides, while some are stick-shaped. Others look like they have pieces of string looped around them. One very common virus is shaped like a spaceship.

Some basic steps can be taken to reduce the spread of viruses. People who have a cold or the flu should cover their mouths with a tissue when coughing or sneezing to help prevent others from getting the virus. They should also wash their hands before having contact with food or with other people.

In addition, vaccines can be administered against some viruses. While a vaccine cannot cure a virus in someone who already has it, a vaccine can prevent a virus from infecting a person who doesn't have it yet. Vaccines teach the body how to produce proteins, called antibodies, which can intercept the virus in the bloodstream. An antibody acts like a key, which fits the keyhole on the virus and locks it up. Some groups of people do not have antibodies against some diseases and other people do. Because they didn't have the matching antibodies, many of the first people who lived in the Americas in the 1600s were killed by viruses carried across the ocean by Europeans. In the current century, many people do have antibodies against the virus that causes AIDS, and thus they don't become ill even though they are infected. Yet, these infected people can still infect other people, some of whom might not have the antibodies.

An entirely new strain of a virus may appear even when a tiny change occurs in its genetic code, or instructions. The virus's genetic code can change rapidly, and it can significantly change the virus's shape. When the shape of the virus changes, the antibody key is no longer able to lock up the new virus. Because of this, vaccines often have to be updated frequently to prevent new waves of infection.

Our ability to see and understand viruses and bacteria has greatly increased in just the last twenty-five years. However, no matter what defenses we create, the genetic codes of viruses and bacteria are easily changed and create new problems for us to try to solve.

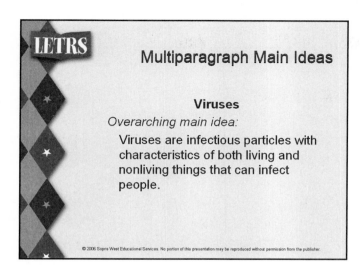

Slide 40

Suggestions for multiparagraph main ideas.

A multiparagraph selection will have an overarching main idea that is supported by paragraph main ideas. In the "Viruses" example, the overarching main idea is "Viruses are infectious particles with characteristics of both living and nonliving things that can infect people."

Introduce multiparagraph main ideas by using reading selections containing six to eight paragraphs, such as the "What Is a Mammal?" and "Viruses" selections. Your selection can be a segment from a textbook chapter or an article that is being used to support a class lesson. In textbooks, the section or topic main idea is often provided in bold print. If it is not, follow this progression to determine the paragraph main ideas and the overall topic idea of the selection.

1. Identify the main ideas of each paragraph.

2. Combine and compare these main ideas and determine what they have in common.

3. Develop a phrase or sentence that captures the topic main idea.

Teachers should have students identify section and paragraph main ideas in increasingly longer reading selections. As they develop skill, students can begin using a two-column format to list the main ideas. The main ideas are placed in the left column of the notes.

longer the passage, less likely each paragraph will have own main idea

Slide 41

More techniques for finding the main idea.

1. Goldilocks Technique

The Goldilocks Technique is one of three strategies that students can use to help identify and state main ideas. In the story *Goldilocks and the Three Bears*, Goldilocks discovers that when she sits on the bears' beds, one is too hard, one is too soft, and one is just right. When she tastes the bears' soup, one is too hot, one is too cold, and one is just right. Similarly, when students state a main idea, sometimes it is too general or too specific; it needs to be improved until it is just right. Students should ask themselves these questions as they formulate main ideas:

1. Is my main idea too general?

2. Is my main idea too specific?

3. How can I change it so it is just right?

The following examples include main idea statements that are too general, too specific, and just right from the readings used in this section.

Paragraph 1:

In the movies, the life of a pirate seems adventurous and exciting. In reality, however, it was difficult and dangerous. The pirates did not eat well because fresh food rotted quickly. They ate mostly hardtack (a dry, plain biscuit) and dried meat, which didn't give them much nutrition. Water often went bad, forcing the pirates to drink beer and rum instead. Many pirates got food

poisoning or seasickness. The ships had no toilets and smelled terribly.

Too general: Pirate life

Too specific: Pirates had to drink beer and rum.

Just right: Pirate life was difficult.

Paragraph 2:

Light passes through the epidermis to reach inner cells known collectively as *mesophyll*. The cells of the mesophyll are where almost all photosynthesis takes place. The shape and arrangement of the upper cells maximize the amount of photosynthesis that takes place. The many air spaces between the cells of the lower layer allow carbon dioxide, oxygen, and water vapor to flow freely.

Too general: Photosynthesis

Too specific: Mesophyll cells

Just right: The internal structure of a leaf promotes photosynthesis.

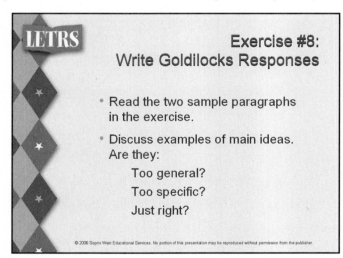

Slide 42

Exercise #8: Write Goldilocks Responses

- ◆ Read the following two paragraphs.

- ◆ Create a main idea for each paragraph that is too general, too specific, and just right for each paragraph.

Paragraph 1:

There was a war game that we little boys played after a big hunt. We went out a little way from the village and built some grass tepees, playing we were enemies and this was our village. We had an advisor, and when it got dark he would order us to go and steal some dried meat from the big people. He would hold a stick up to us and we had to bite off a piece of it. If we bit a big piece, we had to get a big piece of meat, and if we bit a little piece, we did not have to get so much. Then we started for the big people's village, crawling on our bellies, and when we got back without getting caught, we would have a big feast and a dance and make kill talks, telling of our brave deeds like warriors. Once, I remember, I had no brave deed to tell. I crawled up to a leaning tree beside a tepee and there was meat hanging on the limbs. I wanted a tongue I saw up there in the moonlight, so I climbed up. But just as I was about to reach it, the man in the tepee yelled "Ye-a-a!" He was saying this to his dog, who was stealing some meat too, but I thought the man had seen me, and I was so scared I fell out of the tree and ran away crying.

Too general: _____

Too specific: _____

Just right: _____

Paragraph 2:

Born in Italy in the middle of the 13th century, Marco Polo was part of a wealthy merchant family. His father and uncle had already been trading extensively with Middle Eastern countries. They traded silk, porcelain, and other exotic goods over the Silk Road. The Silk Road was a trading route established between China and Rome. As a result, the Polos traveled a great deal. Marco did not meet his father until he was 15 or 16, when his father returned to Venice after many years of travel. This time, when he left again, he took young Marco with him.

Too general: _____

Too specific: _____

Just right: _____

The Goldilocks Technique is easily modeled in class. Ask students to identify the main idea of a paragraph. Record several of their answers on a blackboard or overhead transparency. Through class discussion, analyze each statement to see if it needs to be more specific or more general. It will become apparent that there is no single, best way to state a main idea; there may be several equally good ways of stating it.

2. Labeling the Bucket Technique

A second technique that can be used to identify and state the main idea is a visual representation of the process for finding the main idea. Students are shown a picture of a bucket, or asked to create a mental picture of one similar to the example provided.

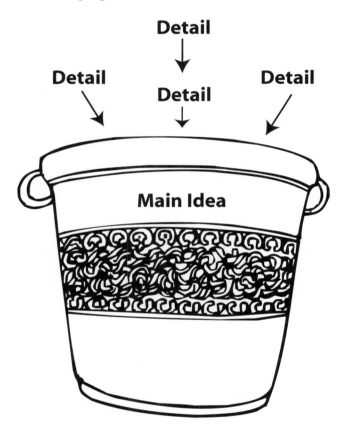

Students should think about the main idea as a label on the bucket that describes as specifically as possible the details inside the bucket. For categorizing, the details are individual words, and the bucket label is the category. For paragraphs, the sentences are the details, and the bucket label is the paragraph main idea. For multiparagraph selections, the paragraphs are the details, and the bucket label is the main idea of the selection.

3. Self-Cueing Technique

Self-cueing questions make up the third technique for identifying and stating main ideas. First, students identify the general topic of a paragraph or multiparagraph selection; then they complete the following statements to identify the more specific main idea:

◆ The topic is _____.

◆ The paragraph is saying this about the topic: _____

_____.

For example, the topic of the following paragraph is "Thanksgiving." Asking what the paragraph is saying about Thanksgiving helps students to identify the main idea, which is "the history of the Thanksgiving celebration" or "celebrating Thanksgiving, then and now":

Thanksgiving falls on the fourth Thursday of November. It began when the Pilgrims invited the Native Americans to a feast. The Pilgrims wanted to thank the Native Americans for helping them grow food and hunt. Today we celebrate Thanksgiving by eating a feast with our families, and we give thanks for the good things in our lives. We eat some of the same foods that the Pilgrims and Native Americans ate many years ago at their Thanksgiving feast.

Another example of self-cueing is "Get the Gist" questions adapted by the Texas Center for Reading and Language Arts (2002):

1. Who or what is the paragraph about?

2. Tell the most important thing about the "who" or the "what."

3. Tell the main idea in ten words or less.

Here are some additional questions that a student can ask to help identify and state the main idea:

1. Are there any words or phrases that are repeated throughout the paragraph or selection? If so, this may suggest the topic.

2. What do all the sentences have in common?

3. Is there a topic sentence that states the main idea? If so, copy or paraphrase it.

4. Do all the key details support the main idea you have stated?

5. Check the main idea by asking if it is too general or specific.

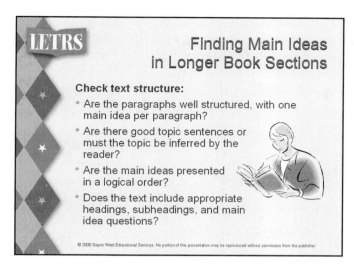

Slide 43

Suggestions for main ideas in textbooks and lengthy selections.

Many students get "lost in the details" when they are reading several pages or more. Reviewing the main ideas before reading provides a big picture and a structure for processing and organizing all the details. Most textbooks include unit and chapter titles, section headings, and subheadings. Sometimes the main ideas are well-represented in these headings and subheadings; however, sometimes a text is not structured. Teachers should preview reading assignments to determine how much structure is provided and how readily the main ideas can be discerned. If the text is well-structured, teachers can simply use the topics and headings in the textbook. If the material is not well-structured, the teacher may have to develop a list of appropriate headings and subheadings. To determine the level of structure, ask these questions:

1. Are the paragraphs well structured, with one main idea per paragraph?

2. Are there good topic sentences, or do they have to be inferred?

3. Are the main ideas presented in a logical order?

4. Does the text include appropriate headings, subheadings, and main idea questions?

The best format for presenting a pre-reading list of headings and subheadings is to use a topic web (see Activity 1 in Part IV).

Suggestions for main ideas in lesson plans.

Many students have difficulty seeing the big picture from daily lessons and individual assignments. They do not make connections between what is taught from week to week. It is helpful for teachers to develop and distribute an overall outline or topic web that will be covered during a unit of study. The topic web can be revisited as the class proceeds through the daily lessons and again at the end of the unit. The topic web is a main idea planner that will also help teachers stay on-task.

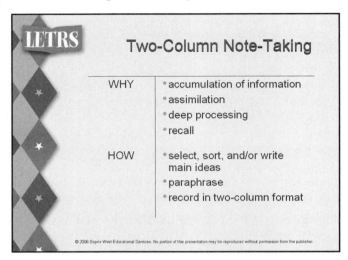

Slide 44

C. How to Teach Note-Taking

Note-taking is a procedure for recording and assimilating information from reading, lectures, or class lessons. Note-taking is a valuable strategy to use during reading so that information will be processed more thoroughly, organized, and remembered. Note-taking is most effective when students express ideas in their own words, paraphrasing information in the text. It is also a valuable tool for gathering and organizing information for a report or research paper.

Note-taking, especially from lectures, is a difficult task for many students. Note-taking is a mental juggling act, as students must hold information in working memory, sort and extract the main ideas to be remembered, select key phrases to write, translate the words into writing or typing, and divide their attention between what they are writing and what the lecturer continues to say. Note-taking from reading is easier and should therefore be introduced and practiced before students are expected to take notes independently from lectures. When students take notes from reading, they can go over the information several times at their own pace. Students in high school will have more confidence in their ability to take lecture notes if they have already mastered note-taking from reading. Basic note-taking instruction can begin in second and third grade, and it should be a major focus in middle school grades.

Two-column format.

The key to note-taking is identifying main ideas and details, paraphrasing them using as few words as possible, and recording them in a structured format. In the late 1970s, Joan Sedita and her colleagues at Landmark School adapted for middle school and high school students the following two-column format based on Walter Pauk's Cornell System for taking notes (Pauk, 1997; Sedita, 1989, 2003).

A page of two-column notes has a vertical line down the page with a horizontal line at the top, forming a T-shape. The vertical line is placed approximately 1/3 of the page width from the left border. The two-column format provides a clear visual distinction between main ideas (listed in the left column) and key details (listed in the right column). A heading or topic for the notes is included in the space at the top of the page above the horizontal line. The example below provides a visual of this format and can be shared with students.

Sample Note-Taking Format

	Heading or Topic
(Topic-Level or Paragraph-Level Main Ideas)	**(Details)**

Several of the seven Key Three activities in the last section of this module include two-column notes; each is a variation of the basic format. In Activity 3, topic (section) ideas are listed in the left column, and paragraph main ideas constitute the details in the right column. In Activities 4A and 4B, paragraph main ideas are listed in the left column, and details from sentences are in the right column.

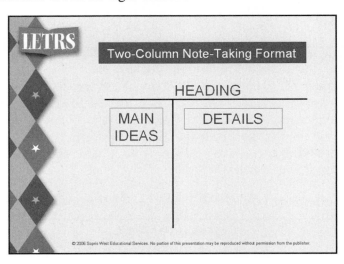

Slide 45

Two-column notes are more effective than using outlines or graphic organizers. In a classic outline, the visual distinction between main ideas and details is limited to five-space indentations. When students go back to review outlines, the notes appear as a steady stream of words. Students once again get lost in the details. Although a graphic organizer offers a good visual distinction between main ideas and details, in order to set up a page for notes, students must know ahead of time how many main ideas and submain ideas there will be. Also, if more than one page of notes is taken, students lose the advantage of seeing how pieces of information are related on the page. Two-column notes offer the best visual and practical layout of main ideas and details. They are also more efficient to use for studying. The details in the right column can be covered while the student reads each main idea and tries to remember the details. Likewise, the main ideas can be covered while the student uses the details to remember the main topics.

Exercise #9: Two-Column Notes About Mammals

♦   Reread the "What Is a Mammal?" passage on page 56–57.

♦   Complete the two-column notes that have been started (below) on the mammals passage. Note in the right column the important details for each subtopic listed in the left column.

Mammals

First mammals on Earth	– 200 million years ago – evolved from extinct group of reptiles – were very small
Different types of mammals	– 4000 types of mammals – all have certain things in common
Three things in common	– warm-blooded vertebrates – have hair or fur – feed young with milk from mammary glands
Importance of hair and fur	– acts as insulation in cold climate
Mammals are warm-blooded	– can survive cold climate – internal temperatures stay the same
Circulatory system	– four-chambered heart and blood vessels – heart pumps blood to lungs to get oxygen – heart then pumps blood to all parts of the body
Excretory system	_____
Nervous system	_____
Senses	_____

Exercise #9 (continued)

Reproduction _____

_____

_____

Three types of reproduction _____

_____

_____

Teachers of all grades need to provide models of two-column notes. In order to meet the needs of students with a wide range of note-taking abilities, teachers can create several versions of a set of notes, including:

♦ **A blank template**—Students must identify all the main ideas and key details.

♦ **A partially completed template**—The teacher provides the main ideas and students must identify the details, or vice versa.

♦ **A complete set of notes**—The teacher provides a complete set of notes for students to use to edit and complete their own notes. A complete set of notes will also assist struggling readers.

Note-taking can be taught to whole classes at once. The class reads a section of a passage as a group. The teacher then asks students to identify the main ideas and details and writes them on the board or an overhead transparency. Students can also work in small groups, sharing their ideas about what they think is important to note and the best way to phrase the notes.

An open-book quiz is one way of encouraging students to take complete notes. Students can use their notes to answer main idea and detail questions; credit is given for a correct answer only if the answer can be located in the notes.

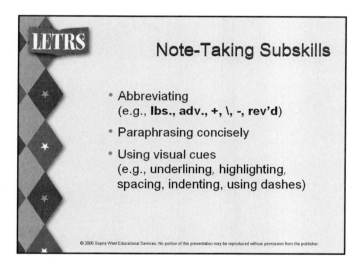

Slide 47

Slide 48

Note-taking subskills.

There are three subskills that students must possess to be efficient note-takers:

♦ Abbreviating

♦ Paraphrasing, using concise wording

♦ Using visual cues to edit notes.

Abbreviating may seem to be a basic skill, but many middle school and high school students do not know how to abbreviate. Teachers should directly teach and model how to apply abbreviations for taking notes. They should demonstrate how the meaningful parts of words (morphemes) form the basis for abbreviations (e.g., "Eng" for *England*; "trans" for *transport*), and acquaint students with commonly accepted abbreviations (e.g., "w/" for *with*, "+" for *and*). When modeling note-taking on the board, teachers can ask students to suggest abbreviations.

Paraphrasing main ideas into concise phrases is another subskill that should not be taken for granted. It is ironic that just when students have reached fifth grade and have learned to write in complete sentences, they must switch to condensing their ideas into phrases for notes. Model how to paraphrase by "thinking aloud" your word-choice decisions. Have students practice condensing sentence-type notes into simpler phrasing.

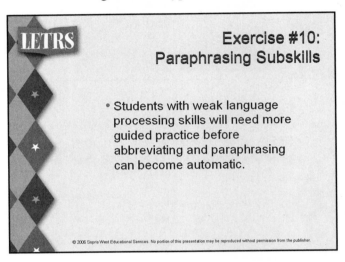

Slide 49

Exercise #10: Paraphrasing Subskills

- Each of these short activities builds the subskills that lead to more efficient and precise use of one's own words to take notes.

1. Substitute words for the underlined words:

   Hurricane Ivan <u>caused a lot of damage</u> when it <u>passed through</u> Mobile.

2. Mark nouns (**N**), verbs (**V**), adjectives (**adj**), and adverbs (**adv**):

   Brain studies consistently have shown that orthographic input stimulates medial extrastriate regions in the posterior left cerebral hemisphere.

3. Find and circle the simple subject and the main verb in this sentence:

   Many of the colonies, rich in valuable natural resources, funneled wealth back into the British Empire.

4. Condense these three sentences into one sentence by combining the subjects and predicates:

   Marco was released from prison. The next year, he returned to Venice. He died there in 1324.

Preskills? purpose to see organization of complex sentence

Finally, some students need to be shown how to add visual markers—especially when reviewing and editing notes—to provide more visual organization to the page. Some examples of visual markers include:

◆ Drawing horizontal lines across the page after each main idea to visually "chunk" the notes.

◆ Using colored markers to highlight important information or to make connections between sections of notes that are related.

◆ Numbering the order of details.

◆ Leaving extra space after each main idea so that there is room to add information that may have been missed.

◆ Adding arrows, stars, or brackets to show connections between or among ideas.

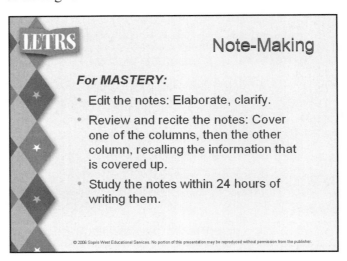

Slide 50

Note-taking vs. note-making.

Note-taking consists of recording information in an organized format, such as two-column notes. *Note-making* consists of active strategies for learning and mastering that information, including editing, reviewing, reciting, and studying notes. Editing steps include:

◆ Check to be sure that all the main ideas are included and are clearly stated in the left column.

◆ Check to be sure that all key details are in the right column. If there is irrelevant information, cross it out.

◆ Ask the teacher or another student to provide missing information.

◆ If wording is excessive, reduce it to concise phrases or sentences.

◆ Expand abbreviations and wording if the notes are unclear.

♦ Add visual markers such as horizontal lines, arrows, numbers, etc., to further organize notes.

♦ Make sure all note pages are dated and in order.

Next, notes should be reviewed and recited. Cover the right column of the notes that contains key details. Review each main idea in the left column and try to remember the details that support it. Similarly, the left column can be covered and the details in the right column can be used to try and remember the main ideas. Editing and reciting should take place as soon as possible after initial notes have been taken, preferably within 24 hours.

Slide 51

Using a two-column format for studying vocabulary.

A two-column format is an efficient and practical format for noting and studying new vocabulary. The words are listed in the left column, and definitions, synonyms, and/or a sample sentence are listed in the right column. Students can fold back or cover either side of the page to study and self-quiz the new vocabulary. See the example below:

Vocabulary for "What Is a Mammal?"	
extinct	Species that once lived on Earth but no longer exist
vertebrates	Species that have a backbone (vertebrae that hold the spinal cord of the nervous system)
mammary glands	Glands, usually on the underside of a mammal, that produce milk for feeding offspring
warm-blooded	Animals that maintain a constant body temperature by their internal chemical reactions to the external temperature

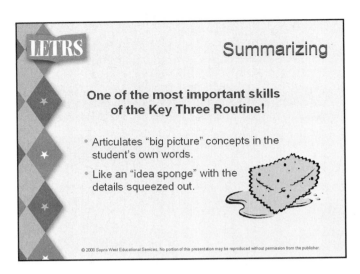

Slide 52

D. How to Teach Summarizing

A summary is an overview of the most important information from a reading selection, class lesson, or lecture. Creating a summary helps students see the "big picture" and compels them to reprocess the information to express it in their own words. A summary is always shorter than the original material, and it does not contain many details. Before a summary can be created, students must first identify key main ideas.

The action of a sponge provides a good metaphor for understanding the summarizing process. The information from which a summary will be generated is heavy with details, like a sponge that is full of water. The information is then reduced to a series of main idea

"Would you please elaborate on 'then something bad happened'?"

phrases, like the sponge after it is squeezed to remove the water. To generate the summary, main ideas are then expanded into sentences, just as the sponge expands somewhat after it is squeezed. The summary is a complete overview of the original, minus the details.

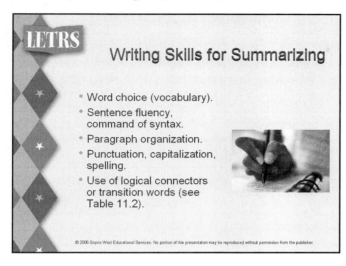

Slide 53

Writing skills.

In order to generate a summary, students must possess basic writing skills including:

♦ The ability to vary word choice, to generate synonyms, and to use appropriate transition words (command of semantics).

♦ The ability to combine sentences, to create compound and complex sentences, to change word order within a sentence, and to apply appropriate grammatical rules (command of syntax).

♦ The ability to develop introductory and concluding sentences, to reorder sentences, and to create new paragraphs when subtopics change (flexibility in discourse organization).

♦ The ability to proofread for spelling, capitalization and punctuation, and content (editing skills).

Transition words (e.g., **before**, **likewise**, **eventually**) are useful for connecting sentences in a summary. Struggling readers often are not adept at using transition words or at using them correctly. They may require examples and guided practice to develop this skill. It is helpful to post a list of transition words in the classroom and to have students keep a list in their notebooks that they can refer to when writing. A list of transition words is provided on the next page in Table 11.2.

Table 11.2. Transition Words and Phrases

Writing Purpose	Appropriate Words / Phrases
To indicate a time relationship	*after, afterward, after that, at first, at this time, before, beginning with, beyond, during, earlier, ending with, eventually, finally, following, from then on, in the meantime, last, later, meanwhile, next, now, since, soon, then, until, while*
To indicate spatial placement	*below, beside, between, beyond, farther on, here, next to, parallel with*
To list or present a series of ideas	*after, after that, finally, first, lastly, next, second, third*
To add information or continue a line of thought	*also, another, besides, further, furthermore, in addition, likewise, moreover, similarly*
To summarize or show conclusion	*accordingly, finally, in conclusion, in other words, in short, to conclude, to sum up, to summarize*
To show comparison	*by comparison, compared to, in like manner, likewise, similarly*
To show contrast	*although, but, however, in contrast, nevertheless, on the contrary, on the other hand, unlike*
To repeat information or stress a point	*above all, in fact, in other words, most important, once again, to repeat*
To provide an example or illustrate a point	*for example, for instance, such as, to illustrate, that is*
To show cause and effect	*as a result, because, because of, caused by, consequently, for that reason, that is why, therefore, thus*
To state the obvious	*certainly, granted that, in fact, most certainly, naturally, obviously, of course, surely, undoubtedly, without a doubt*

Teachers need to distinguish between a student who cannot comprehend the main ideas and a student who is just having difficulty writing about them. Struggling writers may recognize the main ideas, but they may need help with semantic, syntactic, paragraph, or editing skills to write a summary. To help struggling writers, teachers need to point out and reinforce the following writing guidelines:

◆ Details sometimes need to be incorporated to adequately convey a main idea.

◆ Every main idea does not have to have its own sentence. Two related main ideas can be combined into one sentence, or more than one sentence may be required to render a single main idea.

◆ The order of main ideas is flexible once they are taken out of text.

◆ Depending on the length of the original material being summarized, a summary can be a single paragraph or a series of paragraphs.

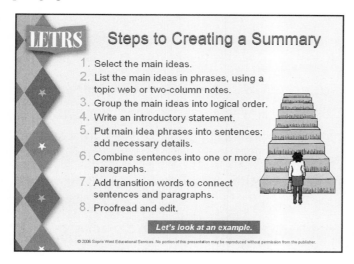

Slide 54

How to write a summary.

This list reviews the steps to writing a summary.

1. Read the material and identify the main ideas. Distinguish the main ideas from the details.

2. Write the main ideas in phrase form. The main ideas can be noted in a list, in a topic web, or in the left column of two-column notes.

3. Group the main ideas into logical categories. Keep in mind that the order in which you identify the main ideas is not always the best order for writing a summary.

4. Begin the summary with an introductory statement.

5. Turn the main ideas into sentences, occasionally including details when it is necessary to convey the main idea.

6. Combine the sentences into one or more paragraphs.

7. Use transition words to connect the sentences and the paragraphs.

8. Proofread the summary for punctuation, spelling, sentence structure, and content.

Summaries can be developed from short reading passages (e.g., a newspaper article) or longer reading selections (e.g., a chapter in a textbook), from both expository and narrative types of text, and from lectures or classroom activities. The following example summary is from the "What Is a Mammal?" passage. Transition words and phrases have been underlined.

Example: Summary from two-column notes
What Is a Mammal?

The first mammals evolved 200 million years ago from reptiles. There are many types of mammals; <u>however</u>, they all have certain things in common. <u>For example</u>, they are warm-blooded vertebrates, they have fur or hair, and they feed their young from mammary glands. Mammals can survive cold climates <u>because</u> of their hair or fur and because their internal temperatures stay the same. Mammals <u>also</u> have highly evolved circulatory, excretory, and nervous systems. Mammals reproduce using one of three methods: egg-laying, bearing young in a pouch, or growing the young internally.

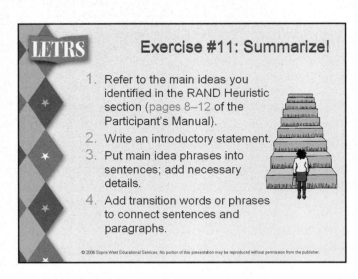

Slide 55

Exercise #11: Summarize!

♦ Write a one-paragraph summary of the RAND Heuristic on pages 8–12.

♦ Use the main ideas and details from the two-column notes you wrote in Exercise #1. Use the main ideas as the basis for your summary.

♦ Underline the transition words and phrases in your summary.

_____

_____

_____

_____

_____

_____

_____

_____

_____

_____

_____

_____

_____

_____

_____

_____

_____

_____

_____

PART IV: Seven Activities for Classroom Application of the Key Three Routine

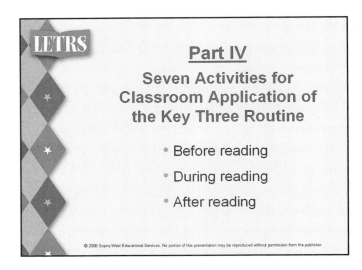

Slide 56

A. Using the Key Three for Comprehension Before, During, and After Reading

Reading and response strategies can be used before, during, and after reading in any content area. The purposes for each application of the Key Three can be delineated by the phase of reading or study activity. Each purpose is consistent with research-supported practices for enhancing reading comprehension (Duke et al., 2004; Kamil, 2004; Pressley, 2000).

Slide 57

Writing: A Road to Reading Comprehension

- ◆ **Before:** To help students see the "big picture" before they start reading and managing details; to activate prior knowledge; to generate a purpose for reading; and to make predictions about what students will learn.

- ◆ **During:** To help students stay focused on reading for a purpose; to process and organize the information they are learning; and to verify or change predictions.

- ◆ **After:** To organize the information learned through reading and discussion; to store the key information so that it can be easily retrieved; and to deepen students' engagement with the information, especially by expressing their understanding of that information in their own words.

The seven activities listed in Table 11.3—and associated terminology listed in Table 11.4—incorporate the Key Three (statement of main ideas, note-taking, and summarizing) into multiple-strategy applications. These can be used for a short reading passage, a lengthy reading selection, a classroom lesson, or an entire unit of study. Students should be asked to apply Key Three strategies before, during, and after reading.

Table 11.3. Seven Key Three Activities for Classroom Application

Key Three Activity	Targeted Comprehension Strategy or Skill	When Used
1. Create a **topic web** to delineate the content or subject matter that is covered in the reading or provided by the teacher.	♦ predicting/pre-reading ♦ graphic organizers ♦ main idea/summarizing	Before, during, after
2. Turn **topics** or **paragraph main ideas** into questions (what do students want to know?)	♦ predicting/pre-reading ♦ main idea/summarizing ♦ generating/answering questions ♦ comprehension monitoring	Before, during
3. Place **topic main ideas** taken from the **topic web** in the left column of **two-column** notes. Read and identify **paragraph main ideas** and place them in the right column.	♦ main idea/summarizing ♦ comprehension monitoring ♦ graphic organizers	Before, during
4A. Identify **paragraph main ideas** and place them in the left column of **two-column notes**. Identify **key details** and place them in the right column. OR 4B. Turn **paragraph main ideas** into questions, and place them in the left column of **two-column notes**. Use **key details** to answer the questions in the right column.	♦ main idea/summarizing ♦ comprehension monitoring ♦ graphic organizers	During
5. Use the left column of **two-column notes** to generate a **summary**.	♦ main idea/summarizing ♦ comprehension monitoring	After
6. Use the **topic web** to generate a chapter or unit **summary**.	♦ main idea/summarizing ♦ comprehension monitoring	After
7. Review and revise **two-column notes**. Use left- and right-column notes to create questions. Answer the questions.	♦ generating/answering questions ♦ comprehension monitoring ♦ graphic organizers	After

Table 11.4. List of Essential Terms Used in the Seven Classroom Activities

Term	Definition
Key detail	A word, a group of words, a phrase, or a sentence that contains an essential, detailed piece of information that supports the main idea.
Paragraph main idea	A single main idea that forms the basis for an individual paragraph. The paragraph main idea is usually explained and supported by key detail sentences in the paragraph.
Topic main idea	The broader main idea of a cluster of related paragraph main ideas (e.g., the main idea of a short article, a section of a chapter, a chapter, or a unit of a book). Topic main ideas can form a hierarchy of main ideas.
Topic web	A graphic organizer that represents the hierarchy of main ideas from a particular article, story, text chapter, daily or long-term lesson, or lecture.
Two-column notes	A note-taking format that lists main ideas in the left column and supporting details in the right column. When taking detailed notes that include paragraph main ideas and key details within the paragraphs, the paragraph main ideas are listed in the left column and the supporting key details are listed opposite the related main idea in the right column. When taking broader notes that include just topic main ideas and paragraph main ideas, the topic main ideas are listed in the left column and the paragraph main ideas are listed in the right column.
Summary	An oral or written overview, in the student's own words, of the key concepts from a reading, lecture, class lesson, or unit of study. A summary is comprised primarily of paragraph and topic main ideas connected by transition words and phrases. A summary contains few details.

B. Teaching and Applying the Seven Activities

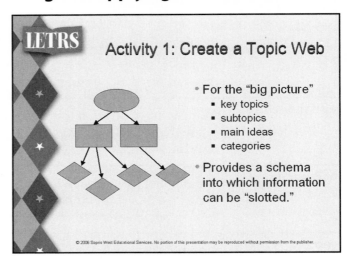

Slide 58

Activity 1: Create a Topic Web

◆ Create a **topic web** to delineate the content or subject matter that is covered in the reading or provided by the teacher.

Students often begin reading without first stepping back to mentally frame the context and purpose for their reading. Consequently, they may lose sight of the main ideas, focus excessively on details, and become overwhelmed by too much information. Likewise, teachers sometimes begin a lesson or a unit of study without presenting the "big picture" in which the information is to be understood. Some teachers assume that students will develop their own background knowledge and sense of context or that the "big picture" study guides that may be provided in the textbook (e.g., a list of main idea questions in a sidebar or a graphic organizer at the beginning of a chapter) are sufficient for supporting comprehension. On the contrary, many students require direct instruction with models provided by the teacher in order to visualize the conceptual background into which new information is to be assimilated.

Activity 1, in which students create a topic web, is a strategy for creating a "big picture" or visual overview of a topic domain. The graphic organizer is based on a flowchart layout. Key topics, subtopics, and (later) main ideas are organized on a chart inside a series of boxes, circles, and other shapes. They are arranged in a way that emphasizes the relationship of each topic to the others. For example, a topic web for this module is included in the Introduction section, and a partially completed topic web for teaching the seven Key Three activities is included in Exercise #12.

Writing: A Road to Reading Comprehension

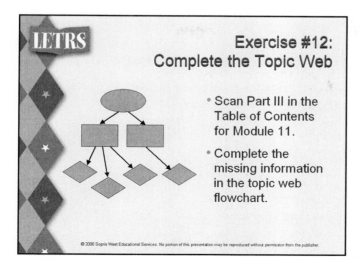

Slide 59

Exercise #12: Complete the Topic Web

♦ This is an incomplete topic web for Part III of this module (pages 39–83).

♦ Scan Part III in the Table of Contents to identify the missing topics.

♦ Fill in the blank flowchart.

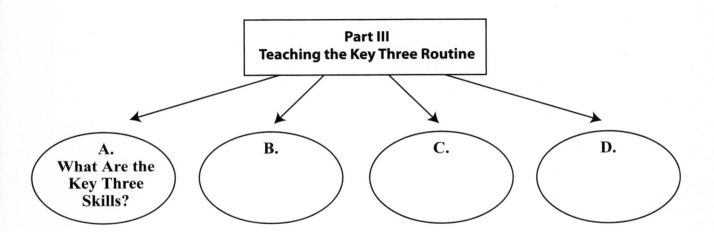

A topic web is a tool for providing an overview of what is to be learned, not for taking notes or focusing on details (see Activities 3, 4A, and 4B for taking notes). A topic web can be generated for a single reading assignment (e.g., a chapter in a book, or a section of that chapter), for a classroom lesson, or for an entire unit of study. Interestingly, many teachers discover that using topic webs helps them keep their lessons organized and focused, and the webs provide a structure for developing quizzes and tests.

The following example is a topic web based on the "What Is a Mammal?" selection on pages 56–57.

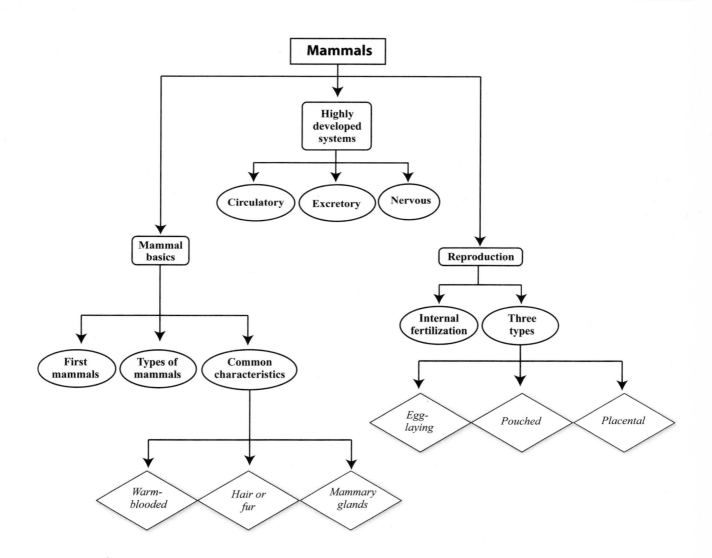

This next example is from a unit of study in a seventh-grade math class.

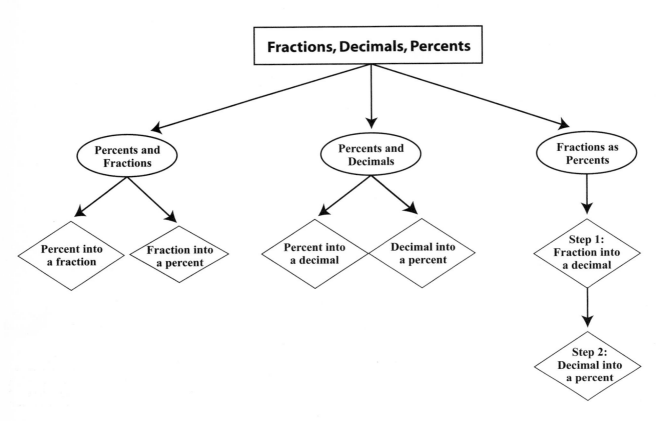

Sources for topic selections.

When a topic web is developed for a unit of study, the topics and subtopics may be generated from headings and subheadings in the textbook that forms the basis for the unit. If a textbook is not being used, a teacher will have to provide a topic web generated from his/her course outline. It is usually easier to generate a topic web when a structured, well-organized textbook is used as the basis for content instruction, but a textbook is not required to use topic webs. Some examples of sources for developing a topic web include:

♦ A unit, chapter, or section of a chapter in a social studies, science, or math textbook.

♦ The main events in a biography.

♦ The elements (e.g., setting, characters, plot) from a literary work such as a short story or a novel.

♦ A series of concepts taught through a series of science experiments.

♦ A schema for studying the elements of poetry.

◆ A schema for organizing, learning, and studying components (e.g., vocabulary, grammar and syntax, cultural perspective) in a foreign language unit.

◆ The main points from a class lecture.

A topic web can represent a unit of study, and additional webs can represent segments of that unit of study. The first example below was generated from a ninth-grade American history chapter. The second example was generated from one section of that chapter.

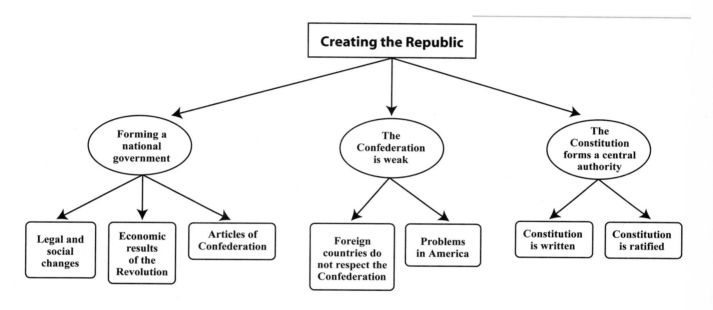

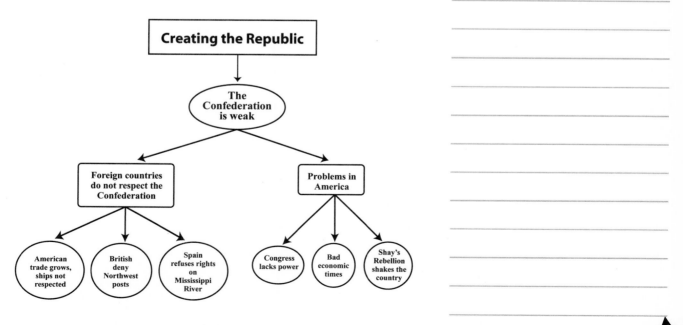

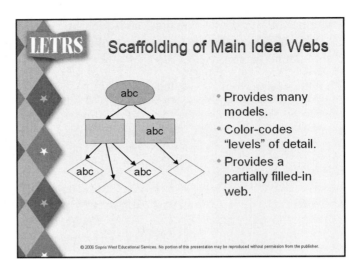

Slide 60

Teacher- and student-generated topic webs.

Initially, teachers need to generate and provide examples of topic webs until students have reached a point at which they can develop the webs independently. Even though students can become proficient at creating webs in one grade, many will continue to need teacher-generated examples as they progress through higher grades, where material is more challenging. Also, students will learn and master strategies at different rates. Teachers can scaffold their instruction for topic and main idea webs by providing webs at various stages of completion to meet different student learning needs.

The first example on the next page illustrates a partially completed topic web for the "What Is a Mammal?" selection (students must determine *some* of the main ideas). The second example on page 96 illustrates the Mammal topic web as a blank template (students must determine *all* of the topic main ideas).

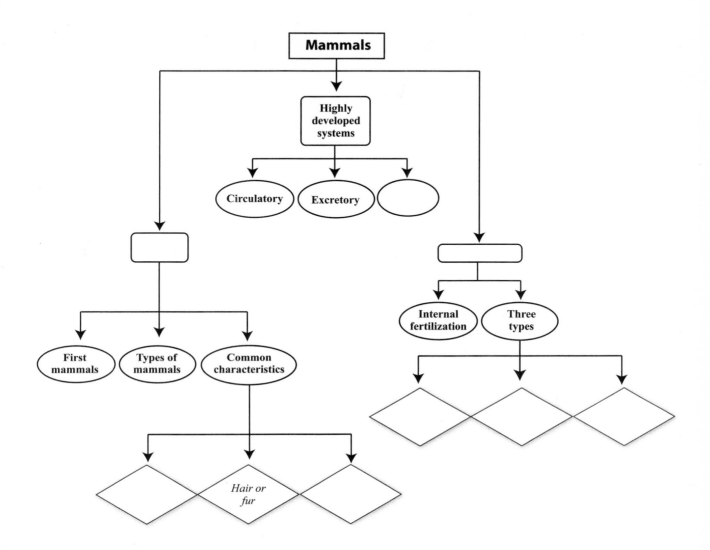

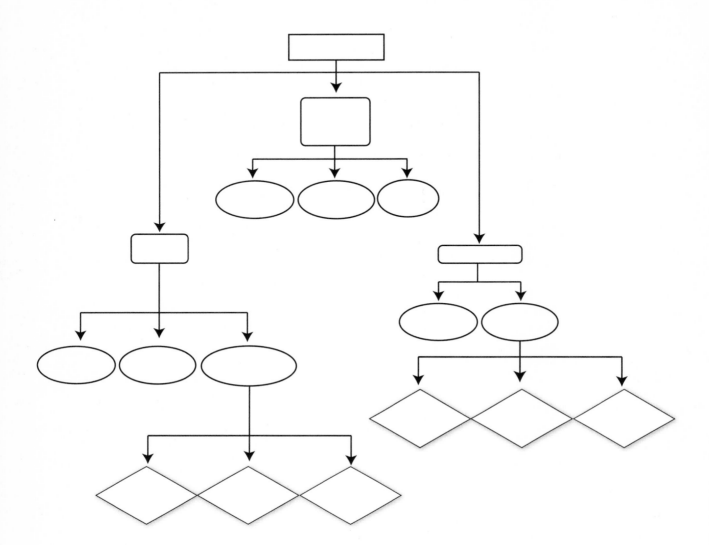

Topic or main idea webs can be generated on a single page of paper, on a poster, or on a blackboard. An overhead transparency can be useful when teachers want to demonstrate how a topic or main idea web can be developed. Software for creating graphic organizers—such as Inspiration® (www.inspiration.com/home/cfm)—can simplify the task but is not necessary.

Using topic webs before, during, and after reading.

Used as a previewing activity, creating a topic web before reading enables students to set goals for reading and to activate prior knowledge. Previewing helps students determine where to focus attention during reading (Brody, 2001). Before reading, a topic web helps students recognize the structure and organization of the text and enables them to create a mental overview of the information.

During reading, comprehension is enhanced when readers construct mental representations in their memory (Texas Center for Reading and Language Arts, 2002). Those mental pictures involve not only descriptive images but also images of the relationships among ideas. Such mental images help students to understand processes or events in the text and to remember abstract concepts (Gambrell & Bales, 1986). The topic web should be reviewed at various points while reading or during a unit of study in order to help students pull back from the details and determine how those details fit in with the "big picture." Using a topic web also "chunks" information into manageable units that can be learned in sections and then pieced together back into the big picture.

Finally, a topic web can be used as an after-reading strategy. It can serve as a general study guide, enabling students to once again step back to see the big picture. The topics and subtopics identify specific units instead of an overwhelming list of details, making it possible for students to organize a study plan.

Using color, size, and shape to demonstrate relationships among ideas.

As noted, a topic web is a visual representation of how topics and subtopics are related in a reading selection, class lesson, or unit of study. The relationship of those ideas can be emphasized and illuminated when different colors, sizes, and shapes are used to generate the web. The size and shape for each topic level in the flowchart should be the same. For example, chapter sections might be listed in large squares just under the chapter title, and subsections might be listed in medium-sized circles, using a smaller size print.

Color can also be used to emphasize the relationship of ideas in a web. For example, each chapter section might be assigned and highlighted a different color, and all the subtopics that fall under that section could be highlighted the same color. Color-coding helps to visually separate different strands of the web. Alternatively, one color can be used for the major topics going across the web, another color for all the subtopics, and yet another color for the smallest-level main ideas. This device helps emphasize the hierarchy of topics and main ideas. Teachers can ask students to bring three different colored ink pens (blue, black, red) to class and use them to copy teacher-generated webs or to create their own webs. Another option is to drag different colored highlighters over sections of the web.

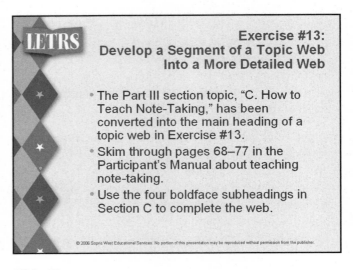

Slide 61

Exercise #13: Develop a Segment of a Topic Web Into a More Detailed Web

- ◆ The section topic "C. How to Teach Note-Taking" has been converted into the main heading of the web below.

- ◆ Skim the pages in this module about teaching note-taking (pages 68–77). Use the four bold-faced subheadings to complete the web.

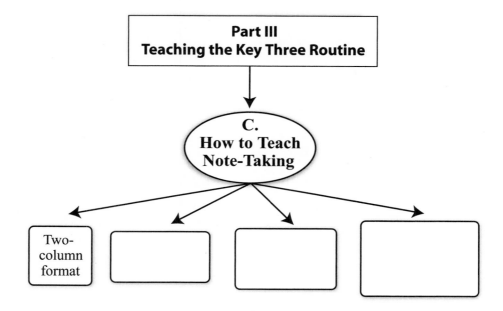

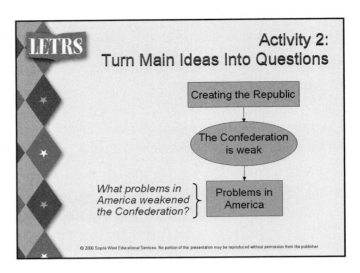

Slide 62

Activity 2: Turn Main Ideas Into Questions

◆ Turn **topic main ideas** or **paragraph main ideas** into questions. What do students want or need to know?

"If I may, Mr. Perlmutter, I'd like to answer your question <u>with</u> a question."

Learning how to generate and answer questions improves comprehension. Students read with greater purpose when they are reading to answer questions, and the generation of questions while reading is a proven technique for promoting active processing of information and ideas. Activity 2, turning topic main ideas or paragraph main ideas into questions, is an activity that compels students to create and answer questions before and during reading. For this activity, each topic or subtopic on the topic web is turned into a question. These questions can be written directly on the topic web, pulled out into a list or placed in the left column of two-column notes. Questions can also be created from paragraph main ideas. These questions can be pulled into a list, or placed in the left column of two-column notes. The following are examples of questions that would address the topics in the "Creating the Republic" topic web.

Example: *Questions that address topics in the "Creating the Republic" topic web*

1. **When** and **why** was the first American national government formed?

2. **List** some of the legal and social changes at that time.

3. **Describe** the economic results of the Revolution.

4. **What** were the Articles of Confederation?

5. **Provide examples** of foreign disrespect for the Confederation.

6. **What** problems in America weakened the Confederation?

7. **Compare** and **contrast** the Constitution with the Articles of Confederation (i.e., how were they the same, and how were they different?).

In Activity 4B (following), you will practice turning paragraph main ideas into questions.

Teaching students to generate and answer questions.

Generating questions does not come naturally to many students. Some students can generate simple "who," "what," "when," "where" types of questions, but they have difficulty generating the more complex "how"

and "why" questions or essay questions that require longer answers based on critical thinking. Teachers must continually model how to generate complex questions and provide examples before students can develop this skill independently. Teachers should provide direct instruction in how to turn topic main ideas and paragraph main ideas into questions. This instruction should include the following:

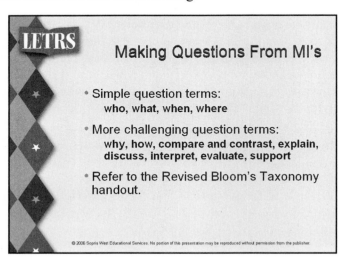

Slide 63

◆ Teach the meaning and use of key question terms (e.g., *demonstrate, compare and contrast, evaluate, explain, relate, discuss, support, interpret*).

◆ Teach how to recognize and use transition and signal words when searching for and generating answers. (e.g., *in addition, however, for example, gradually, consequently, finally, although*).

◆ Teach that there is a continuum of questions ranging from simple "remember" questions through "understanding" and "evaluating" questions (Anderson & Krathwhohl, 2001).

Using main idea questions before, during, and after reading.

Before reading, students can use the main idea questions to activate their prior knowledge and set a goal for reading. This activity can be assigned for homework as a pre-reading strategy. Whether they are generated by the teacher as a class activity or by students, the questions should be discussed, and students can generate predictions about what they expect to learn in order to answer the questions.

During reading, students should be encouraged to search for information that will help them answer the questions. They also should determine if their predictions were accurate and adjust their ideas accordingly. Finally, after reading, students can do a final check to see if their predictions were

correct, and they can use the questions and answers to study for a quiz or test.

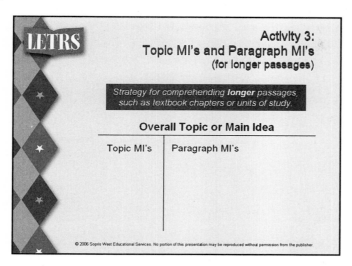

Slide 64

Activity 3 involves the linking of topic main ideas, as identified above, and the main ideas in each paragraph of the selection.

Activity 3: Topic MI's and Paragraph MI's (for longer passages)

♦ Write **topic main ideas** in the left column of two-column notes.

♦ Read and identify **paragraph main ideas**, then write them in the right column.

Once students begin to read and learn information during class, they need an organized way of processing, keeping track of, and remembering that information. Some students get lost in the details and lose track of the main concepts. Some students become overwhelmed by too much information, and others cannot stay focused long enough to remember the information from the beginning to the end of the reading. Activity 3 compels students to interact with the information and provides a structure for taking notes while reading.

The two-column format of these notes enables students to separate, identify, and recall the *topic main ideas* and the *paragraph main ideas* that support them. Activity 3 addresses overall topics and main ideas, not specific details. It is best used for lengthy reading selections (e.g., textbook chapters) and units of study. When students must learn, organize, and remember details, they should shift to using Activities 4A and 4B, which are better for shorter reading selections or individual class lessons.

To accomplish Activity 3, students place a topic main idea in the left column of the two-column notes (the topic main ideas can be pulled from the topic web). Next, they read the paragraphs that support the topic and identify the main ideas of each paragraph. Some main ideas will be stated somewhere in the paragraph, and some will have to be inferred (see Part III, Section B). Students may need to stop every few paragraphs to reflect and get the gist of the main ideas. Sometimes paragraphs do not adhere to conventional paragraph structure, so students cannot assume that every paragraph will contain one main idea. As the paragraph main ideas are identified, they should be written in the right column of the notes, opposite the topic they support. Once a segment of text has been read, students place the next topic main idea in the left column, and repeat the process to determine the paragraph main ideas.

The example below uses the topic main ideas from the second "Creating the Republic" topic web (see page 93). "Foreign countries do not respect the Confederation" is a topic, and there are three subtopics: "American trade grows, ships not respected," "British deny Northwest posts," and "Spain refuses rights on Mississippi River." In the textbook, several paragraphs follow each subtopic. In the example below, the subtopics are listed in the left column, and the paragraph main ideas are listed in the right column.

Foreign countries do not respect the Confederation[8]	
American trade grows, ships not respected	– start of American trade with China brings American ships to Asian waters – despite trade treaties with several countries, American ships do not command respect – American ships and sailors were captured in the Mediterranean – British were hostile and showed only contempt for Americans – Canadian and West Indian ports were closed to American ships
British deny Northwest posts	– Britain refused to turn over Northwest trading posts in American territory – enabled Canadian fur traders to strengthen alliances with Northwest Indians – British found excuses to break treaty agreements
Spain refuses rights on Mississippi River	– Spain possessed Florida and mouth of Mississippi River – Spain refused to let American farmers use port of New Orleans without paying taxes – Americans had to pay the taxes to avoid angering Spain – Jefferson hoped that America would gain strength and Europe's internal quarrels would become an advantage to America

[8] From *America: The Glorious Republic* by Henry F. Graff. (1986). Boston: Houghton Mifflin.

Taking two-column notes while reading compels students to stay focused, to monitor their comprehension, to re-read portions of the text they do not understand, and to state the information in their own words. A review of these notes will remind them of the main points of the reading and how those points are organized into sections of the text.

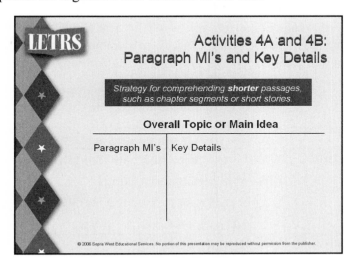

Slide 65

Activity 4A: Identify Paragraph Main Ideas and Key Details

◆ Identify **paragraph main ideas** and write them in the left column of two-column notes.

◆ Identify **key details** and write them in the right column.

OR

Activity 4B: Answer Questions With Key Details

◆ Turn the **paragraph main ideas** into questions, and write them in the left column of **two-column notes**.

◆ Use **key details** to answer the questions in the right column.

Like Activity 3, Activities 4A and 4B use the two-column format for taking notes. These activities, however, focus on identifying and organizing details that support main ideas.

In Activity 4A, students place paragraph main ideas in the left column of the notes. These main ideas can be pulled from Activity 3 notes or generated while reading a selection for the first time. While reading, students also identify all relevant, key details in the paragraphs and write them in the right column. As noted in Part III, Section B, students should paraphrase the main ideas and details in their own words and enter them as phrases rather than complete sentences. The example below lists several paragraph main ideas from the "What Is a Mammal?" reading passage in the left column. The details are listed in the right column.

Example of two-column notes with paragraph
main ideas in the left column

Mammals: Highly developed systems	
Circulatory	– four-chambered heart and blood vessels
	– heart pumps blood to lungs
	– carbon dioxide exchanged for oxygen
	– blood pumped throughout body
Excretory	– highly developed
	– kidneys filter waste from blood into urea
	– urea combines with water to make urine
	– urine travels to bladder and passes out of body
Nervous	– highly developed brain
	– used for thinking and learning
	– highly developed senses such as seeing, hearing

Exercise #14 uses a reading selection titled "Sherpas." The exercise provides an opportunity to practice using two-column notes with the paragraph main ideas in the left column and the supporting key details in the right column.

Sherpas[9]

High in the mountains of Nepal, the Sherpas live in the Khumbu Valley. This valley is considered the southern gateway to Mt. Everest. Sherpas are best known for their climbing prowess and excellent guidance to Everest climbing expeditions. But they have their own culture and customs apart from that as mountain guides.

Traditionally, Sherpas have made their living through trade and agriculture. They herd yaks, a large shaggy mammal similar to a buffalo. The yak fur provides wool for clothing, the hide provides leather for shoes, and the dung (manure) provides fuel for cooking as well as fertilizer for agriculture. The Sherpas drink the yak's milk. They also make it into butter and cheese.

The Sherpas used to trade with Tibet, across the Nangpa La Pass. They would drive their yak herds across the 19,000-foot pass, carrying buffalo hides and other items. They would return with salt and wool. But trade of goods across the pass has almost completely stopped because of the Chinese occupation of Tibet.

The Sherpas also grow food. Potatoes, which can still grow well at high altitutdes, are one of their staples, or basic foods. Potatoes are mixed with meats and vegetables to form a stew. This stew, along with lentils and rice, is their primary meal. Sherpas drink lots of tea, often sweetened with a great deal of sugar and milk.

The Sherpas practice a sect of Buddhism known as *Nyingmapa* Buddhism. Because of their religious beliefs, the Sherpas have always honored the mountains of their region as the homes of gods and goddesses. For example, the Sherpas believe that Mt. Everest, known as *Chomolungma* in the Tibetan language, is the home of the goddess of humans and prosperity. For centuries, the Sherpas kept the mountains sacred by not climbing them. But the allure of Westerners and their money tempted the Sherpas to accept climbing as part of their culture. For modern religious ceremonies and festivals, the Sherpas often gather at the famous Tengboche Monastary, located 16,000 feet up the north side of Mt. Everest.

The Sherpas speak a language that is related to modern Tibetan. But the two languages have grown to be more and more different from each other over the years. This makes communication between the two groups very difficult. Only parts of the language are mutually comprehensible. The languages grew apart for two reasons. First, the Sherpa language is not standardized, meaning that the rules of the language are not written down or formally recognized. Second, the Sherpa

9 Archer, A., Gleason, M., & Vachon, V. (2004). *REWARDS Plus: Application to social studies* (Teacher's Guide, pp. 188–189). Longmont, CO: Sopris West Educational Services. Used with permission of the authors and publisher.

language does not have a written alphabet. Some people are trying to introduce a written script into the Sherpa language; however, the script would be based on the Tibetan alphabet. Many feel that the Sherpas would not accept the script because it might not represent the language spoken by the Sherpas.

In 1921, some Englishmen made the first expedition to climb Mt. Everest. Sherpas were hired to help them. By the 1970's, mountaineering had become a substantial industry for the Sherpas. Many will travel from their villages to the cities, where the foreign climbing expeditions will hire local guides. The Western climbers have influenced the Sherpa culture. Many Sherpa men now wear Western-style clothing. The Sherpa culture and spirituality have influenced the climbers. But not all effects of mountaineering have been positive for the Sherpas.

Western influences, such as deforestation and litter, have become major problems in the Sherpa region. Large numbers of trees have been cut down to make way for new settlements and more agriculture and to be used as fuel in the form of firewood. Everest base camp, the starting point for Everest expeditions, was littered with used oxygen bottles, garbage, and other evidence of the many climbers. However, recent efforts to clean up base camp and lower regions of Everest have succeeded. In 1976, the Khumba region was declared a national park. The national park staff and other Sherpa groups have also begun to manage the forests and other natural resources. These efforts will help ensure that the Sherpas can continue to maintain their culture and heritage and to preserve their traditions and region.

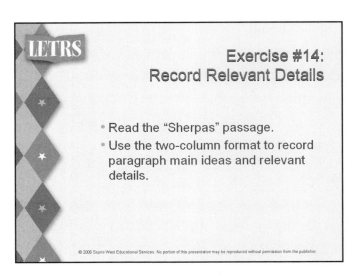

Slide 66

Exercise #14: Record Relevant Details

◆ Read the "Sherpas" passage and identify the paragraph main ideas.

◆ List the paragraph main ideas in the left column of the two-column note-taking template provided below.

◆ Then, record relevant details in paraphrases (your own words) in the right column, making a list rather than writing in complete sentences.

Sherpas

Paragraph Main Ideas	Relevant Details

Exercise #14: Record Relevant Details (continued)

Paragraph Main Ideas	Relevant Details

In Activity 4B, students turn the paragraph main ideas into questions, which are then placed in the left column of two-column notes. The details are used to answer the questions in the right column of the two-column notes. The example below turns several paragraph main ideas from the "What Is a Mammal?" reading passage used in Part III, Section B. The details are used to answer the questions in the right column.

Example of two-column notes with paragraph main ideas turned into questions

Mammals: Highly developed systems	
Describe the circulatory system.	Mammals have a four-chambered heart that pumps blood to the lungs to exchange carbon dioxide for oxygen. This oxygen-rich blood is pumped to all parts of the body through blood vessels.
How do mammals excrete?	Mammals have a highly developed excretory system. Kidneys filter waste from the blood and turn it into urea. Urea combines with water to make urine, which travels to a bladder and passes out of the body.
How does the nervous system work?	Mammals have the most highly developed brain of all animals. It makes thinking and learning possible. The nervous system also provides senses, such as seeing and hearing.

In Exercise #15, you will use the "Sherpas" passage to practice turning paragraph main ideas into questions and then use details to answer the questions.

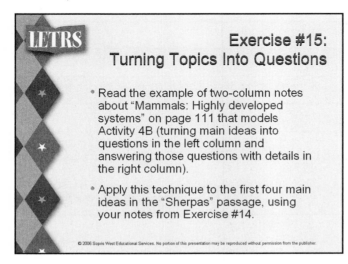

Slide 67

Exercise #15: Turning Topics Into Questions

♦ Using the notes you took in Exercise #14, turn the first four paragraph main ideas in the "Sherpas" passage into questions, and write them in the left column.

♦ Use the details to answer the questions in the right column.

Sherpas

Main idea questions	Details as answers

As in Activity 3, taking two-column notes while reading compels students to be active readers, to monitor their comprehension, and to express the details in their own words.

Adapting Activities 3, 4A, and 4B to meet different student needs.

These activities can be adapted to meet a range of note-taking abilities within a classroom. Advanced readers can be asked to discern all of the main ideas and details on their own and determine where to write them in the two-column notes. Students who still need some support before they can complete the activity independently can be given a set of notes that are partially completed. Teachers can provide all of the main ideas, all of the details, or some of both. Finally, for struggling readers, teachers can provide a complete set of notes to help guide students while they read.

Activities 3, 4A, and 4B can also be used to guide study or synthesis of information after reading. Students can fold over or cover the right side of the notes and use main ideas and questions on the left side to quiz themselves. Similarly, they can cover the left side and use the details to quiz for the main ideas.

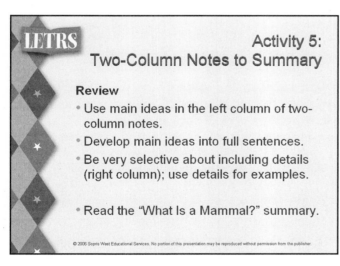

Slide 68

Activity 5: Two-Column Notes to Summary

◆ Use the left side of **two-column notes** to generate a **summary**.

"This has merit, but could you go back through and add more 'like's and 'you know's?"

Earlier in this module, we described what a summary is, why it is important, and how to teach students to create summaries.

Activity 5 is to be completed after reading. Two-column notes that were generated from Activity 4A are used as the understructure for the summary, particularly the paragraph main ideas from the left column. The first sentence of the summary is an introductory sentence that identifies the general topic that the paragraph main ideas support. Then, each main idea is developed into a main idea sentence.

Because a summary is an overview of main points, most of the details in the right column should not be included in the summary. Sometimes, however, a detail is needed to make a main idea sentence more meaningful and complete; a detail can provide an example. Transition phrases such as *for instance*, *to illustrate*, and *for example* are useful for connecting the detail to the main idea sentence.

In the example below, two-column notes that were taken from the "What Is a Mammal?" passage (see pages 56–57) were used to generate a summary. Transition words and phrases are underlined.

Example of a summary from two-column notes
What Is a Mammal?

The first mammals evolved 200 million years ago from reptiles. There are many types of mammals; <u>however</u>, they all have certain things in common. <u>For example</u>, they are warm-blooded vertebrates, they have fur or hair, and they feed their young from mammary glands. Mammals can survive cold climates <u>because</u> of their hair or fur and because their internal temperatures stay the same. Mammals <u>also</u> have highly evolved circulatory, excretory and nervous systems. Mammals reproduce using one of three types of internal fertilization: egg-laying, pouched, or placental.

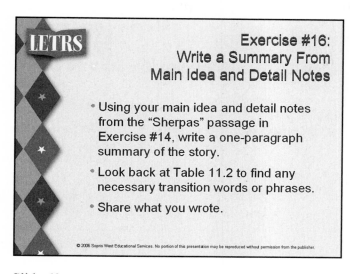

Slide 69

Exercise #16: Write a Summary From Main Idea and Detail Notes

◆ Using your main idea and detail notes on the "Sherpas" reading (Exercise #14), write a one-paragraph summary of the passage.

◆ Link your sentences with well-chosen transition words and phrases from Table 11.2 on page 80.

◆ Compare your summary with those of your colleagues.

_____

_____

_____

_____

_____

_____

_____

_____

_____

_____

_____

_____

_____

_____

_____

A summary that is generated from paragraph main ideas should embody the proposition structure in the passage, without adding interpretive statements. This type of summary would be used for a single reading selection (e.g., an article, an essay, a section of a chapter). Class lessons can be summarized in the same way. To generate a summary from a broader scope of information (e.g., a textbook chapter, a unit of study), a series of Activity 5 summaries can be connected. Another option for longer selections is to use Activity 6 below.

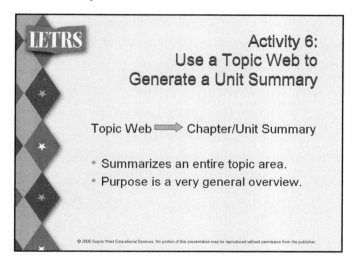

Activity 6:
Use a Topic Web to
Generate a Unit Summary

Topic Web ⟹ Chapter/Unit Summary

• Summarizes an entire topic area.
• Purpose is a very general overview.

Slide 70

Activity 6: Use a Topic Web to Generate a Unit Summary

♦ Use the **topic web** to generate a chapter or unit **summary**.

A topic web, as in Activity 1, can also serve as the understructure for a summary of a whole chapter or unit of study. This type of summary begins with an introductory sentence that identifies the overall topic, which is usually located at the top of the flowchart. Next, topics from the second tier of the web are developed into one- to three-sentence sections of the summary. Main ideas from the remaining tiers are used to add detail to these sentences, and transition words are used to connect the summary sections. An Activity 6 summary is more general than an Activity 5 summary; it is best used as a tool to summarize an overview of a topic area.

Color-coding sentences according to the level of topic detail they represent is a useful strategy for concretizing the role of each sentence. *Step Up to Writing* (Auman, 2002) is an approach to teach expository writing that uses color-coding of sentences extensively.

In the following example, the topic web for this LETRS module (see page 4) was used to generate a summary of this module. Once again, transition words and phrases are underlined.

Example: A summary of a large segment of text
Writing: A Road to Reading Comprehension

The purpose and goal of this module is to present a model for comprehension strategy instruction, <u>including</u> reading and writing skills, for use in intermediate, middle school, and high school grades. Participants first take the Pretest, then scan a topic web for an overview of the module. The module <u>begins</u> by explaining why strategy instruction is important. The causes of comprehension problems are reviewed, <u>as well as</u> the research findings on effective strategy instruction. The role of vocabulary and language structures in comprehension is explained. <u>Next</u>, the module emphasizes the importance of active responding to improve comprehension across all content areas. <u>In addition</u>, the module provides suggestions for how to teach three key skills using both narrative and expository text. The three skills <u>include</u> identifying and stating main ideas, note-taking using a two-column format, and summarizing. These skills are <u>then</u> combined into a series of seven activities, <u>also known as</u> the Key Three Routine. The activities can be used before, during, or after reading. Suggestions for teaching each of the seven activities are provided, <u>along with</u> examples from history, math, and science content classes. <u>Finally</u>, recommendations are given for integrating this strategy instruction model on a schoolwide basis.

The summaries of Activities 5 and 6 are important written responses that can consolidate information from a passage or unit of study. To write a summary, students must review and reflect on the information they have learned, and then express that knowledge in their own words. Writing necessitates the active learning that supports long-term memory of information. When students write summaries, they also gain confidence that they can adequately demonstrate and express their knowledge.

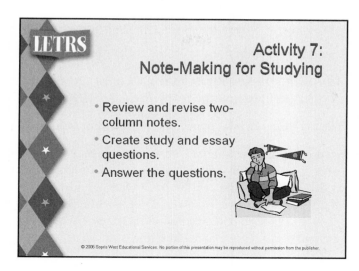

Slide 71

Activity 7: Note-Making for Studying

◆ Review and revise two-column notes.

◆ Use the left and right columns to create study and essay questions.

◆ Answer the questions.

Earlier, we distinguished *note-making* from *note-taking*. This is the point at which students progress from capturing key main ideas and details in text to gaining control over information in the service of new learning. Although the act of discerning main ideas and details and paraphrasing them in note-taking is, in itself, an essential process for comprehending and organizing information, note-making activities necessitate command over subject matter and the ability to use it to extend one's thinking process to generate new ideas.

The first step to note-making is to edit two-column notes to be sure they are complete and easy to read. As noted in Part III, Section B, editing steps include:

◆ Check to be sure that all main ideas are included and clearly stated in the left column.

◆ Check to be sure that all key details are in the right column. If there is irrelevant information, cross it out.

◆ Ask the teacher or another student to provide missing information.

◆ Reduce wording into concise phrases for the sake of brevity.

◆ Expand abbreviations and wording if the notes are unclear.

◆ Add visual markers such as horizontal lines, arrows, or numbers to further organize notes.

◆ Make sure that all note pages are dated and in order.

Next, the two-column notes should be reviewed, recited, and studied. Students can cover the right column of the notes (which contains key details), review each main idea in the left column, and try to recall the covered details that support it. Conversely, students can cover the left column of the notes (which contains main ideas), review the details in the right column, and try to restate each main idea associated with the details. If Activity 4B notes were taken, the main ideas have already been turned into questions in the left column, and the answers in the right column include the key details.

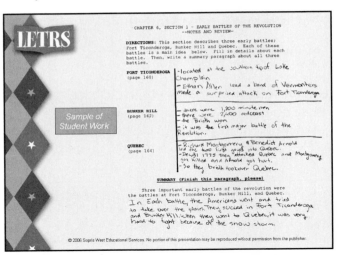

Slide 72

Finally, students develop questions from both the left and right columns of the notes that extend thinking at the higher levels of analysis, synthesis, interpretation, or evaluation. They generate the types of open-ended questions that might be asked on an essay test. They write the answers in complete sentences, referring to the notes to be sure the answers are complete, but adding more interpretation and evaluation statements. In addition, specific facts that need to be memorized as well as new vocabulary can be pulled from the notes onto study cards.

Similar to summarizing, Activity 7 is an important strategy for integrating information and gaining intellectual command over it. Note-editing, review and study, and answering questions from notes compels students to actively engage with the information. For additional suggestions about note-making activities, see Part III, Section B.

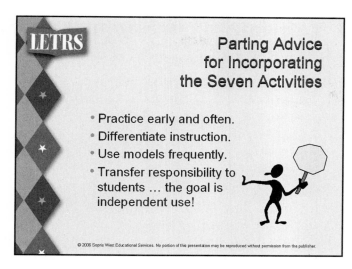

Slide 73

Some final words about using the seven activities.

The comprehension skills and strategies presented in this module should be taught repeatedly over the span of several grades. The degree to which teachers introduce, model, and provide guided practice with the seven activities will vary, based on students' abilities, the content subject, and the level of difficulty of the material. Part of the teacher's role is to determine when assistance is needed and when it is appropriate to push students to take responsibility for applying strategies independently.

Generally, students need a significant amount of modeling and practice before they can internalize reading, writing, and study strategies. If students are introduced to strategy instruction before fifth or sixth grade, they will have some tools to address the more challenging reading and classwork in middle school, and they can build a base of comprehension strategies to bring into high school. If *all* teachers in a grade or a school promote strategy instruction, students will receive the practice they need over a shorter period of time.

Sometimes teachers have trouble determining how much they should do for students and how much students should do for themselves. Given the demands on teachers in grades five and above to cover significant amounts of content before the end of each term, they can be tempted to generate the main idea web, two-column notes, summaries, and study questions for students. Although this may provide easier access to the content, in the long term, students will not learn how to apply strategies on their own.

The goal for strategy instruction is for students to gradually take on responsibility for incorporating comprehension and writing strategies. It is important to identify when a student is ready to apply each of the seven activities, and when he or she still needs support from the teacher.

PART V: Schoolwide Support of the Key Three Routine

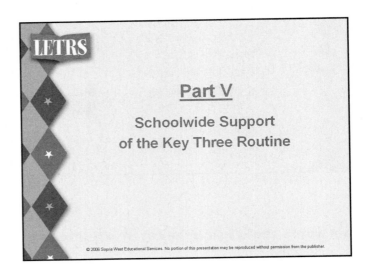

Slide 74

A. Conditions for Achieving Sustainable Schoolwide Implementation

Achieving schoolwide implementation of comprehension, writing, and study strategies across all content-area instruction is possible if certain conditions are established. Strategy instruction can be part of a school-wide literacy program, implemented across all content areas, among teachers in every grade. The following schoolwide conditions facilitate the most effective use of the approaches taught in this module.

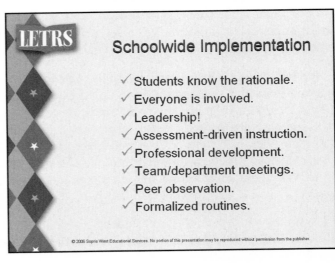

Slide 75

♦ Students learn the rationale for what they are learning. Parents are also informed.

♦ **All** professional and paraprofessional staff members are involved in implementation.

♦ Leadership provides ongoing support and guidance to implement strategy instruction:

  ● Administration is aware and committed.

  ● There is common planning time for communication between same-grade teachers and multigrade teachers.

  ● The schedule accommodates groups with a range of reading instruction needs.

  ● Student groupings are flexible; membership is periodically reevaluated.

♦ Assessment drives instruction:

  ● General screening is in place to identify good readers and struggling readers.

  ● Diagnostic assessment provides specific guidance for struggling readers.

  ● Progress-monitoring occurs with comprehension, study, and writing strategies.

♦ Professional development is sufficient for all professionals and paraprofessionals because it:

  ● Includes overview of the reading acquisition process.

  ● Gives reasons for integration of comprehension, study, and writing strategies into content-area instruction.

  ● Teaches how to teach reading comprehension, writing, and study strategies.

  ● Provides follow-up training for long-term implementation, including observation and feedback in the classroom.

♦ Team and department meetings are devoted to implementing the Key Three and other learning and study techniques:

  ● A grade-level meeting or departmental meeting convenes at least once a month.

  ● Teachers share their implementation of Key Three seven activities and support one another.

♦ Peer observation provides a safe context in which to learn new skills:

  ● The classroom teacher develops a lesson plan that includes a Key Three activity.

  ● A goal for that plan is shared with the observer *before* the observation.

- After the observation, an opportunity to discuss the lesson is scheduled.

◆ The routines are formalized:

- Develop and distribute a description of the model and how it is being implemented in the school.

- Make sure new students and teachers are given an overview of the model.

- Communicate with teachers of students in earlier grades so they know the kind of strategy instruction their students will receive when they move on to the next grade.

- Communicate with teachers in the grades that your students will graduate to so that they can continue the strategy instruction.

- Give student, parent, and teacher surveys midway or at the end of the first year of the program to provide feedback on the reaction of the school community to the model.

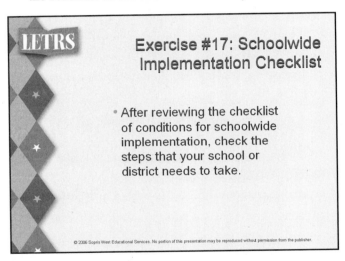

Slide 76

Exercise #17: Schoolwide Implementation Checklist

♦ Using the guidelines stated on pages 123 and 124, check the steps or procedures that you need to undertake in your school or district in order to achieve schoolwide implementation of the Key Three Routine.

_____

_____

_____

_____

_____

_____

_____

_____

_____

_____

_____

_____

_____

_____

_____

_____

_____

_____

_____

_____

_____

_____

_____

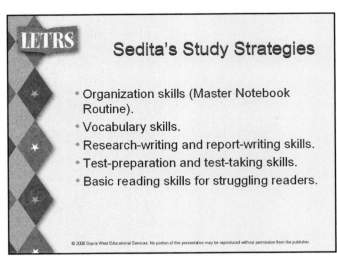

Slide 77

Now, revisit the questions in the Pretest. Are you more confident of your responses? What are three teaching strategies that use writing to enhance reading comprehension you will remember and apply?

1. _____

2. _____

3. _____

Slide 78

B. Additional Strategies for Schoolwide Implementation

Organization skills.

Many students do not have the organization skills necessary to develop and maintain a system for organizing their class papers, homework, notebook and school supplies, or assignments. Good organization skills go hand-in-hand with comprehension and study skills. Organization skills help students structure their spatial, temporal, and material worlds and the information they must learn.

Students need direct instruction and modeling to develop a consistent routine for organization. The Master Notebook Routine, developed by Joan Sedita (1999), is a model for maintaining a "working notebook" and a systematic approach to sorting, filing, and saving class and homework assignment, notes, handouts, and other key papers. The Master Notebook Routine also includes a daily and long-term calendar routine for planning homework and long-term assignments.

Schoolwide implementation of an organization skills model such as the Master Notebook Routine ensures that students receive consistent instruction and guided practice that is reinforced as the student moves from class to class and grade to grade. The model needs to be flexible to accommodate different teaching styles, yet structured enough so that students see a consistent approach for applying organization strategies.

(For more information about the Master Notebook Routine, see the reference to the STRATEGIES series in Appendix A.)

Vocabulary skills.

A schoolwide approach for vocabulary instruction is important because vocabulary knowledge is linked so strongly to comprehension and academic success. Like organization skills, vocabulary instruction goes hand-in-hand with comprehension strategy instruction. Although many teachers incorporate some vocabulary instruction in their individual classes, it is important to develop a schoolwide approach that incorporates consistent instructional practices across all content classes and all grade levels within a middle school or high school.

An effective vocabulary instruction model should include a multicomponent approach to increasing vocabulary knowledge that includes both direct and indirect instruction. *Direct instruction* means teaching specific words, such as a pre-reading list of content words. It also includes instruction in the analysis of word parts, such as roots and affixes. *Indirect instruction* includes exposure to new words through wide reading and helping students develop an appreciation for words.

General strategies for teaching vocabulary are presented in LETRS, Module 4. In addition, a schoolwide approach for vocabulary instruction is included in Sedita's (2003) Key Three routine instruction model.

Research- and report-writing skills.

In order to write a good research report, students must have well-developed organization skills, comprehension strategies (including note-taking and summarizing), and writing skills. In addition, most students need direct instruction in how to combine these skills to the specific task of producing a research report. There is a process, or series of steps, that must be taught, modeled, and practiced before students can independently complete a research report. Specifically, they must learn how to:

- ◆ brainstorm, narrow, and select a topic and subtopics

- ◆ search and use information from various sources such as books, articles, and the Internet

- ◆ read for comprehension and identify information that is relevant to the research topic

- ◆ take notes and organize information into outlines before writing

- ◆ produce first and final drafts

- ◆ assemble footnote information and construct a bibliography.

Many students are overwhelmed at the prospect of completing a research report. However, teaching and modeling the research process as a series of manageable steps provides direction and confidence. It is helpful to provide numerous opportunities to practice those steps, which is why it is better to assign a series of short research projects over the school year rather than one large paper.

Middle schools and high schools should develop a schoolwide plan for introducing basic report-writing skills, gradually increasing the difficulty of the projects as students progress through the grades. A standard model for assigning projects and providing time lines, researching, taking notes and developing outlines, and referencing sources should be adopted by *all* teachers in a school.

(For more suggestions on how to develop a schoolwide model for research and report-writing, see the reference to the STRATEGIES series in Appendix A.)

Test-preparation and test-taking skills.

Many students perform poorly on classroom tests because they do not have good test-preparation and test-taking skills. They are willing to study, but they do not know how to do so effectively. They may have

adequately mastered the information but are anxious and disorganized during a test, and therefore do not do as well as they could.

Teachers should provide direct, systematic instruction in test-preparation and test-taking skills. Test preparation includes organizing assignments and class work throughout a unit of study (see Master Notebook Routine), developing a study plan for reviewing information over several days, and applying strategies for thinking and writing about the information (see Key Three Routine). Test-taking skills include how to approach a test and establish a plan for completing a test, how to answer certain types of questions (e.g., matching, true/false), and how to structure and write an answer to an essay question.

Once again, middle schools and high schools should develop a school-wide model for providing direct instruction in test preparation and test-taking skills that is consistent among all teachers.

(For more suggestions on how to develop a schoolwide model for teaching test-preparation and test-taking skills, see the reference to the STRATEGIES series in Appendix A.)

Basic reading skills for struggling readers.

There are many reasons why struggling readers have comprehension difficulties, including inadequate development of word recognition, decoding, and fluency skills; weak language-processing skills; limited vocabulary knowledge; and limited life experience and background knowledge. As a result, many struggling readers need direct instruction with supplemental programs that address these specific reading skills deficits. Module 10 of LETRS addresses these professional development needs.

A listing of experimentally and clinically tested programs for poor readers in intermediate, middle school, and high school is included in Appendix A.

Bibliography

Anderson, L. W., & Krathwhohl, D. R. (Eds.) (2001). *A taxonomy for learning, teaching and assessing: A revision of Bloom's taxonomy of educational objectives.* New York: Addison-Wesley Longman.

Auman, M. (2002). *Step up to writing.* Longmont, CO: Sopris West Educational Services.

Barton, M. L., & Heidema, C. (2002). *Teaching reading in mathematics: A supplement to teaching reading in the content areas* (2nd ed.). Aurora, CO: Mid-continent Research for Education and Learning (McREL).

Beck, I. L., McKeown, M. G., Hamilton, R. L., & Kucan, L. (Eds.) (1997). *Questioning the author: An approach for enhancing student engagement with text.* Newark, DE: International Reading Association.

Berninger, V. W., & Richards, T. L. (2002). *Brain literacy for educators and psychologists.* Amsterdam, The Netherlands: Academic Press.

Brody, S. (2001). Comprehension: Gathering information and constructing understanding, and Previews: Learning pertinent background and text concepts. In S. Brody (Ed.), *Teaching reading: Language, letters, and thought* (pp. 213–253). Milford, NH: LARC Publishing.

California Department of Education. (2000). *Strategic teaching and learning: Standards-based instruction to promote content literacy in grades four through twelve.* Sacramento, CA: Author.

Carlisle, J. (1982). *Reading and reasoning (Level 1).* Cambridge, MA: Educators Publishing Service.

Carlisle, J. (1983). *Reading and reasoning (Level 2).* Cambridge, MA: Educators Publishing Service.

Carlisle, J., & Rice, M. (2002). *Improving reading comprehension: Research-based principles and practices.* Baltimore: York Press.

Chall, J. (1996). *Stages of reading development (2nd ed.).* Orlando, FL: Harcourt Brace.

Curtis, M. E., & Longo, A. M. (1999). *When adolescents can't read: Methods and materials that work.* Cambridge, MA: Brookline Books.

Dale, E., & Chall, J. S. (1948). A formula for predicting readability. *Educational Research Bulletin, 27,* 11–20; 37–54.

Dickson, S., Simmons, D., & Kame'enui, E. (1995). *Text organization: Curricular and instructional implications for diverse learners* (Technical Report No. 18). Eugene: University of Oregon, National Center to Improve the Tools of Educators. Retrieved January 10, 2005, from http://idea.uoregon.edu/~ncite/documents/techrep/tech18.html

Duke, N. K., Pressley, M., & Hilden, K. (2004). Difficulties with reading comprehension. In C. A. Stone, E. R. Silliman, B. J. Ehren, & K. Apel (Eds.), *Handbook of language and literacy: Development and disorders* (pp. 501–520). New York: Guilford Press.

Ehri, L. (1996). Development of the ability to read words. In R. Barr, M. Kamil, P. B. Mosenthal, & P. D. Pearson (Eds.), *Handbook of reading research: Volume II* (pp. 383–418). Mahwah, NJ: Lawrence Erlbaum.

Gambrell, L. B., & Bales, R. J. (1986). Mental imagery and the comprehension-monitoring performance of fourth and fifth-grade poor readers. *Reading Research Quarterly*, *21*, 454–464.

Gaskins, I. W. (1998). There's more to teaching at-risk and delayed readers than good reading instruction. *The Reading Teacher*, *51*(7), 534–547.

Grossen, B. (2004). Success of a direct instruction model at a secondary level school with high-risk students. *Reading & Writing Quarterly*, *20*, 161–178.

Harvey, S., & Goudvis, A. (2000). *Comprehension strategies that work.* York, ME: Stenhouse.

Hillocks, G., Jr. (1986). *Research on written composition: New directions for teaching.* Urbana, IL: National Council for Teachers of English.

Hochman, J. (1999). Teaching written composition. In J. Birsh (Ed.), *Multisensory teaching of basic language skills.* Baltimore: Paul Brookes.

Kamil, M. (2004). Vocabulary and comprehension instruction: Summary and implications of the National Reading Panel findings. In P. McCardle & V. Chhabra, (Eds.), *The voice of evidence in reading research* (pp. 213–234). Baltimore: Paul Brookes.

Kamil, M., Rosenthal, P., Pearson, P. D., & Barr, R. (Eds). (2000). *Handbook of reading research* (Vol. 3). Mahwah, NJ: Lawrence Erlbaum Associates.

Klingner, J. K., & Vaughn, S. (1999). Promoting reading comprehension, content learning and English acquisition through collaborative strategic reading. *The Reading Teacher*, *52*, 738–747.

Lenz, K., & Bulgren, J. A. (1995). Promoting learning in content classes. In P. T. Cegelka & W. H. Berdine (Eds.), *Effective instruction for students with learning disabilities* (pp. 385–417). Boston: Allyn & Bacon.

Jacobs, V. (1997). The use of connectives in low-income children's writing: Linking reading, writing, and language skill development. In L. Putnam (Ed.), *Readings on language and literacy: Essays in honor of Jeanne S. Chall* (pp. 100–130). Cambridge, MA: Brookline Books.

Lovett, M. W., & Steinbach, K. A. (1997). The effectiveness of remedial programs for reading disabled children of different ages: Does the benefit decrease for older children? *Learning Disability Quarterly*, *20*, 189–210.

McWhorter, K. T. (1983). *College reading and study skills* (2nd ed.). Boston: Little, Brown and Company.

Meltzer, J., Smith, N. C., & Clark, H. (2002). *Adolescent literacy resources: Linking research and practice.* Providence, RI: The Education Alliance at Brown University.

Meltzer, L., & Montague, M. (2001). Strategic learning in students with learning disabilities: What have we learned? In D. Hallahan & B. K. Keogh (Eds.), *Research and global perspectives in learning disabilities: Essays in honor of William J. Cruickshank.* Mahwah, NJ: Lawrence Erlbaum Associates.

Moats, L. C. (2004). Efficacy of a structured, systematic language curriculum for adolescent poor readers. *Reading & Writing Quarterly*, *20*, 145–159.

National Reading Panel. (2000). *Teaching children to read: An evidence-based assessment of the scientific research literature on reading and its implication for reading instruction. Reports of the subgroups.* Washington, DC: National Institute of Child Health and Human Development.

Oakhill, K., & Cain, J. (1998). Individual differences in children's comprehension skill: Toward an integrated model. In C. Hulme & M. Joshi (Eds.), *Reading and spelling: Developmental disorders* (pp. 343–348). Mahwah, NJ: Lawrence Erlbaum Associates.

Pauk, W. (1997). *How to study in college* (7th ed.). Boston: Houghton Mifflin.

Pearson, P. E., & Gallagher, M. C. (1983). The instruction of reading comprehension. *Contemporary Educational Psychology*, *8*, 317–344.

Peterson, C. L., Caverly, D. C., Nicholson, S. A., O'Neill, S., & Cusenbary, S. (2000). *Building reading proficiency at the secondary level.* Austin, TX: Southwest Educational Development Laboratory.

Pisha, B., & O'Neill, L. (2003). When they learn to read, can they read to learn? *The International Dyslexia Association Perspectives*, *29*(4), 14–18.

Pressley, M. (2000). What should comprehension instruction be the instruction of? In M. Kamil, P. Mosenthal, P. D. Pearson, & R. Barr (Eds.), *Handbook of reading research* (Vol. 3, pp. 545–561). Mahwah, NJ: Lawrence Erlbaum Associates.

Pressley, M., Brown, R., El-Dinary, P. B., & Afflerbach, P. (1995). The comprehension instruction that students need: Instruction fostering constructively responsive reading. *Learning Disabilities Research and Practice*, *10*(4), 215–224.

Rashotte, C. A., MacPhee, K., and Torgesen, J. K. (2001). The effectiveness of a group reading instruction program with poor readers in multiple grades. *Learning Disability Quarterly*, *24*, 119–134.

Roehler, L. R., & Cantlon, D. J. (1997). Scaffolding: A powerful tool in social constructivist classrooms. In K. Hogan & M. Pressley (Eds.), *Scaffolding student learning: Instructional approaches and issues* (pp. 6–42). Cambridge, MA: Brookline Books.

Sedita, J. (1989). *Landmark study skills guide.* Prides Crossing, MA: Landmark School Press.

Sedita, J. (1999). Organization strategies: The master notebook system. *Their World, 1998/1999 Annual Edition.* New York: National Center for Learning Disabilities.

Sedita, J. (2001). *Study skills: A landmark school teaching guide* (2nd ed.). Prides Crossing, MA: Landmark Outreach Program.

Sedita, J. (2002). *STRATEGIES: The master notebook routine.* Boston: Sedita Learning Strategies.

Sedita, J. (2003). *STRATEGIES: The key three routine.* Boston: Sedita Learning Strategies.

Seidenberg, M. S., & McClellan, J. L. (1989). A distributed, developmental model of word recognition and naming. *Psychological Review*, *96*, 523–568.

Snow, C. (2002). (Chair). *RAND reading study group: Reading for understanding: Toward an R&D program in reading comprehension.* Santa Monica, CA: RAND.

Spache, G. (1953). A new readability formula for primary-grade reading materials. *Elementary School Journal*, *55*, 410–413.

Stone, C. A., Silliman, E. R., Ehren, B. J., & Apel, K. (Eds.). (2004). *Handbook of language and literacy: Development and disorders.* New York: Guilford Press.

Stahl, S. A. (1999). *Vocabulary development*. Newton Upper Falls, MA: Brookline Books.

Stahl, S. A., & Fairbanks, M. M. (1986). The effects of vocabulary instruction: A model-based meta-analysis. *Review of Educational Research, 56*(1), 72–110.

Stotsky, S. (2001). Writing: The royal road to reading comprehension. In S. Brody (Ed.), *Teaching reading: Language, letters, and thought* (pp. 276–296). Milford, NH: LARC Publishing.

Swanson, H. L., Hoskyn, M., & Lee, C. (1999). *Interventions for students with learning disabilities: A meta-analysis of treatment outcomes*. New York: Guilford Press.

Texas Center for Reading and Language Arts. (2002). *Teacher reading academies*. Adapted from Klinger, J. K., & Vaughn, S. (1998). Using collaborative strategic reading. *Teaching Exceptional Children, 30*(6), 32–37; and Mathes, P. G., Fuchs, D., & Fuchs, L. S. (1995). Accommodating diversity through Peabody classwide peer tutoring. *Intervention in School and Clinic, 31*(1), 46–50.

Appendix A

Evidence-Based and Research-Based Curriculum Materials for Teaching Older Students to Read and Write[10]

[10]Based on Kevin Feldman's "Biased Bibliography of Resources for Older Struggling Readers." Used with permission of Kevin Feldman. www.balancedreading.com/FeldmanK-6.pdf

Web site for review of research on teaching older students:

http://www.ed.gov/print/about/offices/list/ovae/pi/hs/adollit.html

Content-area instructional strategies for comprehension and study skills:

The *STRATEGIES* series by Joan Sedita. www.seditalearning.com; (978) 887-2844

STRATEGIES is a series of teacher guides and accompanying professional development that addresses essential skill sets for students in grades 5–12. Each *STRATEGIES* component can be adopted by individual teachers, but schoolwide implementation is highly recommended. Titles in the series include:

STRATEGIES: The Key Three Routine (main ideas, note-taking, and summarizing)

STRATEGIES: The Master Notebook Routine (organization skills)

STRATEGIES: Research- and Report-Writing Skills

STRATEGIES: Test-Preparation and Test-Taking Skills

SIM (Strategies Intervention Model). The University of Kansas Center for Research on Learning: www.ku-crl.org; (785) 864-4780

Project CRISS. www.projectcriss.com; (406) 758-6440

Ed Ellis. www.graphicorganizers.com; (205) 339-3704

Teaching Reading in the Content Areas: If Not Me, Then Who? McREL: www.mcrel.org

Reading instructional programs for older, poor readers:

Corrective Reading—Science Research Associates (SRA). Gary Johnson and Zigfried Englemann. (888) 772-4543

LANGUAGE!® by Jane Fell Greene. Sopris West Educational Services: www.sopriswest.com; (800) 547-6747

Wilson Reading System—*Wilson Language* by Barbara Wilson. www.wilsonlanguage.com; (508) 865-5699

Lindamood Phoneme Sequencing (LIPS) Program for Reading, Spelling, and Speech by Lindamood Bell. (800) 233-1819. Also available from Pro-Ed: (512) 451-3246

Reading Is FAME® (Girls and Boys Town reading program) by Mary Beth Curtis and Anne Marie Longo: www.girlsandboystown.org/pros/training/education/FAME_program_obj.asp

REWARDS by Anita Archer, Mary Gleason, and Vicky Vachon. Sopris West Educational Services: www.sopriswest.com; (800) 547-6747

SIPPS (Systematic Instruction in Phonemic Awareness, Phonics, and Sight Words). Developmental Studies Center, John Shefelbine: (510) 533-0213

Read Naturally Strategy by Candyce Ihnot. www.readnaturally.com; (800) 788-4085

Soar to Success (*not* a decoding program). Houghton Mifflin: www.eduplace.com; (888) 892-2377

Writing programs:

Step Up to Writing by Maureen Auman. Sopris West Educational Services: www.sopriswest.com; (800) 547-6747

Matching students to books:

Advantage Learning Systems / *Accelerated Reader:*
www.epi-center.net/software/products/pages/a/accelerated_reader.html; (800) 890-1472

Scholastic Reading Inventory / *Reading Counts:* www.scholastic.com; (800) 724-6527

Degrees of Reading Power® (DRP) BookLink: www.tasaliteracy.com/booklink/booklink-main.html

The Lexile Framework for Reading: www.lexile.com; (888) LEXILES [539-4537]

Technology-based instruction for older, struggling readers:

Lexia Learning Systems / *Reading S.O.S.* (Strategies for Older Students): www.lexialearning.com; (800) 435-3942

SkillsBank: www.skillsbank.com; (800) 725-8430

Scholastic / *Read 180:* http://teacher.scholastic.com/products/read180/; (800) 724-6527

Inspiration® 7.5: www.inspiration.com/productinfo/inspiration/index.cfm; (800) 877-4292

Don Johnston / Start-to-Finish® Readers: www.donjohnston.com; (800) 999-4660

Kurzweil 3000™ (text to speech and study skill features). Kurzweil Educational Systems: www.kurzweiledu.com; (800) 894-5374

Appendix B

Samples of Student Work

Topic Web (Probability)

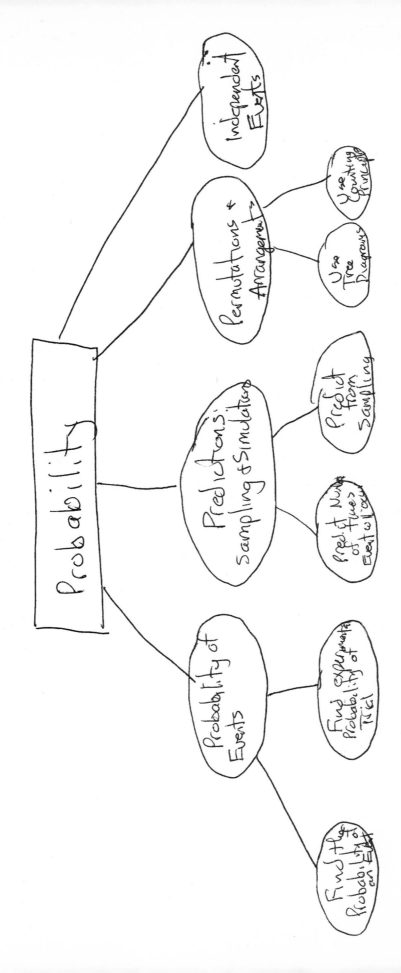

Two-Column Notes: Main Ideas and Details
(Divisibility Rules)

Math # 1
November 19, 2003

Divisibility Rules

Rules for 2:	If the number &2346 / 2342 end in a 0, 2, 4, 6, or 8, there will be divisibility by 2.
Rule for 3:	Add up each individual &1735 / 3805 digit and divide by 3.
Rule for 6:	Both rules for 2 and 3 must work! 82 492 2)492 8436
Rule for 9:	Just like the rule for 3 but add them up, but div. by 9. 9)441 9)3388
Rule of 5:	Last digit must end 0 or 5.

141

Two-Column Notes: Main Idea and Details
(Periodic Tables)

	Periodic Tables Dec 2, 2003
1 Each Element is Identified by Chemical Symbol — (pg 110)	(1) each sqare on the periodic table has the atomic number, atomic mass, name and chemical symbol. Chemical number usually is one to two letters
2 Rows Are Called Periods (pg# 111)	(2) each row (left to right) is called a period. called a period becaus of the reapeating pattern in the elements. Conductivity and election on atom change gradrally from metal to nometal
3 Column are called groups (pg# 111)	(3) From top to bottom element in the periodic table is called a groups elements in some groups often have similar chemical and physical properties somtimes called a group is called a familly.
4 Grouping the elements (pg# 112)	(4) element in the periodic table usally shares similar properties beceause the atom ater layer has the same number in electrons in outer energy levels
5 Groups 1 and 2 Very reactive meatals (pg# 112/113)	elements are reactive because the electrons outer energy level in the atoms. atoms often take, shore, and give electrons which cause coumpound
6 Group 1 Alkali Meatals (pg# 112)	(6) can cut with knife are so low the sodiam potissiam and lithium are less dense then water. most reactive metals
7 Group 2 Alkali earth metals (pg# 113)	are not as reactive because it is harded atoms to give away 2 electrons the to give 1 electron joining with other atom

Two-Column Notes: Questions and Answers

Math	<u>2 Colomn Notes</u>	11/9/03 Per.7
	Measurement	
Why?	food, dwellings, trade, travel, property	
What?	Body parts, sun, moon, stars	
Who?	France	
HOW	Metré - 1670 1800 - Meter convention → daimal Bace 10	

Two-Column Notes: Characters and Details
From the Novel *The Outsiders*

The Outsiders

Johnny Cade greaser	2nd youngest in group Nervous and always a little scared Abuse by his parents The gang takes care of him die from Fire
Sandy greaser	Soda pops girlfriend
Cherry Valance Socs	Red headed cheerleader Bobs girlfriend Friendly with Ponyboy Realises the fighting is wrong
Marcia Socs	Hangs with Cherry Randys girlfriend Friendly with Two Bit
Randy Socs	Bob's Bestfriend Marcia Boy Friend tries to Make peace w/ Ponyboy Realizes fighting is wrong Points out everyone has Problems
Bob Socs	Cherry's Boyfriend Beat up Johnny to begin with Wears rings to fight Spoiled · no rules gets killed by Johnny

Two-Column Notes: Main Ideas, Details Leading to Summary, and Summary
(From a Chapter, "Early Battles of the Revolution")

CHAPTER 6, SECTION 1 - EARLY BATTLES OF THE REVOLUTION
--NOTES AND REVIEW—

DIRECTIONS: This section describes three early battles;
Fort Ticonderoga, Bunker Hill and Quebec. Each of these
battles is a main idea below. Fill in details about each
battle. Then, write a summary paragraph about all three
battles.

FORT TICONDEROGA
(page 160)

- located at the southern tip of Lake Champlain
- Ethan Allen lead a band of Vermonters made a surprised attack on Fort Ticonderoga

BUNKER HILL
(page 162)

- there were 1,200 minute men
- there were 2,400 redcoast
- the Bristh won
- it was the first major battle of the Revolution.

QUEBEC
(page 164)

- Richard Montgomery & Benedict Arnold led the two first goups into Quebec.
- Dec.31 1775 they attacked Quebec and Montgomery got killed and Arnold got hurt.
- So they bristh took over Quebec.

SUMMARY (Finish this paragraph, please)

   Three important early battles of the revolution were
the battles at Fort Ticonderoga, Bunker Hill, and Quebec.
In Each battle, the Americans went and tried to take over the places. They succed in Fort Ticonderoga and Bunker Hill. When they went to Quebec, it was very hard to fight because of the snow storm.

Two-Column Notes: Topic Main Ideas, Details Leading to Summary, and Summary (Hitler)

2 Column Notes

Main ideas	Details
1. Hitler invades Poland	1. - Sept. 1939 - S.U. invades E. Pol. & Baltic States
2. France Surrenders	2. - April 1940 - Ger. invades France, Belgium & Holland - GB trys to help French - Battle of Dunkirk
3. Britsh Prepare for invasion	3. - Winston Churchill Brits: PM. - "Never Surrender"! - Battle of Britain. - Use of radar -

Summary

   In 1939, Hitler attempted to conquer all of Europe. He succeeded with the exception of GB, where WC vowed that they would never surrender.

   in conquering Poland, France, Holland, Belgium, & the Baltic States

Appendix C

Answer Key to Pretest and Exercises

Module 11 Pretest

1. What is the most common underlying cause of reading difficulty in older students (beyond third grade)?

    a. Disinterest in reading.

    (b.) Dysfluent and inaccurate reading of words in print.

    c. Poverty and its general effects.

    d. Fluent reading without understanding.

2. Which of the following is a reading comprehension instruction strategy that is not on the list of research-supported practices?

    a. Writing a summary.

    b. Using graphic organizers before and after reading.

    c. Clarifying misunderstood ideas as reading is taking place.

    (d.) Sustained silent reading during school time.

3. One of the most proven and powerful techniques for introducing children to new vocabulary words is:

    (a.) Embedding each new word in several contextual examples.

    b. Matching definitions to new words before reading.

    c. Asking students to go straight to the dictionary and look up the words.

    d. Concentrating on the most obscure words in the passage.

4. Which of the following statements is **not** true about the relationship among language processing, reading comprehension, and writing?

    a. Taking notes requires awareness of morphology and phrases within sentences.

    b. Stating main ideas requires awareness of the logic of paragraph structure.

    c. Writing a cohesive summary depends in part on the ability to use transition words.

    (d.) Choosing precise vocabulary words is dependent on rapid automatic naming.

Module 11 Pretest (continued)

5. Narrative and expository text differ in which way?

    a. Expository text is always shorter than narrative text.

    (b.) Narrative text is usually centered around a problem that the main character(s) must solve; expository text gives factual support for ideas.

    c. Narrative text is more dense and has more Latin-based words than expository text.

    d. Expository text is designed to tell stories, while narrative text is designed to give information about the world.

6. Which of the following statements is true about paragraph main ideas?

    (a.) Main ideas are often, but not always, found at the beginning of a paragraph.

    b. Main ideas are most often implied and not stated.

    c. In a well-written paragraph, the main idea is stated in the last sentence.

    d. The paragraph main idea is the same as the topic or title.

7. When teachers model comprehension strategies by thinking aloud, they:

    a. Facilitate students' understanding of higher-order comprehension questions.

    (b.) Show students what good readers do to monitor their understanding.

    c. Help students read narrative and expository texts more accurately.

    d. Not sure

8. A student who has an understanding of story structure:

    a. Will have better oral language skills.

    b. Will be better able to understand and recall expository texts.

    (c.) Will be better able to understand narrative texts.

    d. Will be better at making speeches.

Module 11 Pretest (continued)

9. To facilitate comprehension, graphic organizers can be used:

    a. Before reading.

    b. After reading.

    (c.) Before, during, and after reading.

    d. Not sure

10. Main idea webs can be generated from:

    a. Reading stories.

    b. Reading paragraphs.

    c. Reading captions.

    (d.) Reading textbook chapters.

11. Passage summaries are best generated from:

    a. Key words in the subtitles and illustrations.

    (b.) Paragraph main ideas.

    c. The ideas that stand out in memory.

    d. The last sentence in each paragraph.

12. What is the most basic step for finding main ideas?

    (a.) Categorizing

    b. Paragraph level

    c. Multiparagraph level

    d. Not sure

Exercise #1: Reading Comprehension Chart

♦ Major factors that affect reading comprehension are listed in the left column.

♦ List details in the right column, beginning with some of the factors mentioned in the section we've just covered.

♦ Then, feel free to add your own insights into the impact of each of these factors.

Major Factors in Reading Comprehension	Details: Dimensions of Each Factor
Reader/Writer	**Details from the reading:** - brings insight and background knowledge - constructs mental images and models of content - brings learned reading skills: decoding, word knowledge, fluency - has sufficient short-term and working memory - extracts main ideas and makes inferences - makes connections to previous knowledge **Teacher insights:**
Text	**Details from the reading:** - certain text characteristics make a text easier or more difficult to read - surface representation (the language) conveys underlying ideas (the propositions) - texts vary by genre - texts vary by proposition density (number of new ideas) - texts vary in language difficulty at the word and sentence level - some texts more organized than others **Teacher insights:**

Major Factors in Reading Comprehension	Details: Dimensions of Each Factor
Task	**Details from the reading:** – what is the reader supposed to do with the text? – task can affect motivation to read – extrinsic and intrinsic consequences – length of selection – appeal to interest of student **Teacher insights:**
Context	**Details from the reading:** – how much assistance/support is available? – emotional or cognitive support – social context – physical environment **Teacher insights:**

Exercise #2: Three Vocabulary Instruction Techniques

1. **Writing a formal definition.** A formal or classical definition has two parts: Part A names the category to which something belongs or gives a synonym for the word; Part B gives some critical attributes of the concept.

   Example: **Allegiance** is:

   A. loyalty

   B. usually to a social organization, a set of governing principles or a symbol of those principles

   Write a definition for the word **alien** (i.e., citizenship status). _An alien is a person who resides, works, or studies in a foreign country but does not yet have citizenship in that country. An alien can be legal (with a work or study permit) or illegal (with no visa or permit)._

   Write a definition for the term **isosceles triangle**. _An isosceles triangle has three sides, with the angles of two sides that intersect the base being equal._

   Write a definition for the word **ion**. _An ion is a subatomic particle that carries a negative charge._

2. **Scaling words for an attribute.** Construct a scale or continuum showing the relationship of these words to one another:

   disturbance, apocalypse, debacle, catastrophe, disaster, calamity, upheaval, misfortune, ruin

   disturbance, misfortune, upheaval, ruin, disaster, debacle, calamity, catastrophe, apocalypse

Exercise #2: Three Vocabulary Instruction Techniques (continued)

3. **Creating a multiple-meaning web.** Make a web for multiple meanings of the word **right**. In each box, write a phrase that exemplifies the word's use as well as a brief definition of that particular meaning of **right**.

He was considered a **right**-wing candidate.

Definition: Very conservative politically.

She knew her answer was **right**.

Definition: Correct; without error.

right

The streets met at **right** angles.

Definition: With 90 degrees between the intersecting lines.

Turn **right** at the next house.

Definition: The direction opposite of left; toward the right hand.

Exercise #3: Comprehension Strategies and Techniques

◆ List the strategies and techniques you now routinely use to teach comprehension.

Before Reading	During Reading	After Reading

◆ Circle the domain(s) in which you feel you are most effective.

◆ Share with a colleague something you feel is working well to foster comprehension in your classroom as well as something that you feel needs improvement.

Participant answers will vary. Encourage discussion of results.

Exercise #4: Paragraph Play

Part 1:
◆ Given these sentences, which one(s) should be dark blue? Green? Yellow? Light blue?
◆ Rearrange the sentence order according to the color-coded sentence hierarchy.

Dyslexia results from differences in the structure and function of the brain. (dark blue)

Several brain areas are activated in support of normal reading, but the dyslexic brain does not exhibit normal activation patterns on fMRI. (green)

For example, before remediation is successful, the brains of dyslexic students may try to read by relying on the right cerebral hemisphere rather than the left. (yellow)

The dyslexic brain overrelies on the front part of the language (left) hemisphere and is slow to activate posterior regions, which are responsible for fast word recognition. (yellow)

Connections between sounds, symbols, and meanings are hard to establish. (yellow)

Fortunately, brain science also shows that the dyslexic brain can be "normalized" in response to appropriate teaching. (light blue)

Part 2:
◆ Given this topic sentence, write the rest of the paragraph.
◆ Highlight or notate your sentences dark blue, green, yellow, and light blue.

Teaching a class of preadolescent or adolescent students is a job worth $100,000 a year.

(dark blue): Teaching a class of preadolescent or adolescent students is a job worth $100,000 a year. (green): Many highly paid executives do not work under the stress or pressure that teachers do every day. (yellow): First, teachers are the ultimate "multitaskers." (yellow): In addition, they are always "on" in front of large groups of students who present very diverse learning needs. (yellow): Finally, teachers are responsible for the intellectual development of dozens of students and typically work many overtime hours in preparation and nurturing individual students and their families. (light blue): Teaching has its rewards, but pay needs to increase to honor the work that conscientious, professional teachers carry out every day.

Exercise #5: Is the Main Idea Stated or Implied?
◆ Read the following two paragraphs.
◆ Identify the main idea in each paragraph.
◆ Indicate where the topic sentence is located in each paragraph. If there is no topic sentence, write one of your own.

Paragraph 1:

There was a war game that we little boys played after a big hunt. We went out a little way from the village and built some grass tepees, playing we were enemies and this was our village. We had an advisor, and when it got dark he would order us to go and steal some dried meat from the big people. He would hold a stick up to us and we had to bite off a piece of it. If we bit a big piece, we had to get a big piece of meat, and if we bit a little piece, we did not have to get so much. Then we started for the big people's village, crawling on our bellies, and when we got back without getting caught, we would have a big feast and a dance and make kill talks, telling of our brave deeds like warriors. Once, I remember, I had no brave deed to tell. I crawled up to a leaning tree beside a tepee and there was meat hanging on the limbs. I wanted a tongue I saw up there in the moonlight, so I climbed up. But just as I was about to reach it, the man in the tepee yelled "Ye-a-a!" He was saying this to his dog, who was stealing some meat too, but I thought the man had seen me, and I was so scared I fell out of the tree and ran away crying.[4]

Main Idea:

Little boys played war games after a big hunt to prove their bravery.

Topic Sentence:

"There was a war game that we little boys played after a big hunt."

[4]Black Elk. (2000). *Black Elk speaks: Being the life story of a holy man of the Oglala Sioux (as told through John J. Neihardt)*, p. 45. Lincoln, NE: University of Nebraska Press.

Paragraph 2:

Born in Italy in the middle of the 13th century, Marco Polo was part of a wealthy merchant family. His father and uncle had already been trading extensively with Middle Eastern countries. They traded silk, porcelain, and other exotic goods over the Silk Road. The Silk Road was a trading route established between China and Rome. As a result, the Polos traveled a great deal. Marco did not meet his father until he was 15 or 16, when his father returned to Venice after many years of travel. This time, when he left again, he took young Marco with him.[5]

Main Idea:

Marco Polo became a traveler and explorer because his father and uncle included him in the family's merchant trading business.

Topic Sentence:

(None; the main idea is implied. Participant topic sentences will vary.)

[5]Archer, A., Gleason, M., & Vachon, V. (2004). *REWARDS Plus: Application to social studies* (Teacher's Guide, pp. 62–63). Longmont, CO: Sopris West Educational Services. Used with permission of the authors and publisher.

Exercise #6: What Categories Can Be Constructed?
◆ Create categories for these vocabulary words from a sixth-grade unit about ancient Egypt.

amulet: a charm worn to bring good luck

Anubis: the god of embalming and guide for the newly dead

Book of the Dead: a collection of spells/prayers to help with the passage to the afterlife

canopic jars: containers for the internal organs of an embalmed body

cartouche: an oval shape surrounding an inscription of a royal name

cataracts: steep rapids in a river

Delta: the point at which water leaves a river and enters the sea

Giza: the place where the pyramids were built

Hatshepsut: the first female ruler of the New Kingdom of Egypt

Imhoptep: the architect who designed the first pyramid for King Zoser

inundation: the annual flooding of the Nile

Kush: a country to the south of Egypt

Luxor: the place of royal cemeteries

mastaba: a rectangular-shaped tomb with sloping sides and a flat top

Menes: the king who first unified upper and lower Egypt

natron: a mineral/salt used in mummification

obelisk: a tall and thin four-sided stone pillar

papyrus: a water reed that was used for making paper

Pharaoh: the title for the rulers of Egypt

Ra: the first and most important Egyptian god

Red Sea: the sea that borders Egypt on the east

sarcophagus: a stone coffin

Exercise #6: What Categories Can Be Constructed? (continued)

    scarab: an amulet in the form of a beetle

    scribes: professional writers or recordkeepers

    shroud: a cloth in which a dead body is wrapped

    sphinx: a statue with the head of a human and the body of a lion

    tributary: a small river that feeds into the Nile

Possible categories:

People: Hatshepsut, Imhoptep, Menes, Pharaoh, scribes

Places: Giza, Kush, Luxor, Red Sea

Objects: amulet, canopic jars, cartouche, papyrus, sarcophagus, scarab, shroud

Words associated with the afterlife: Anubis, Book of the Dead, canopic jars, mastaba, natron, sarcophagus, shroud

Words associated with the Nile River: cataracts, delta, inundation, tributary

Buildings or monuments: Giza, Luxor, mastaba, obelisk, sphinx

Egyptian gods: Anubis, Ra

One-syllable words: Kush, Ra, shroud, sphinx

Three- or more-syllable words: amulet, Anubis, canopic jars, cataracts, Hatshepsut, Imhoptep, mastaba, obelisk, papyrus, sarcophagus, tributary

---

Exercise #7: Delineating and Coding Main Ideas

◆ Read this article.

◆ Underline the topic sentences, and place symbols in the margin to identify the location and type of main ideas. Watch for paragraphs that should be divided into two because two main ideas are included. Use brackets to divide these paragraphs.

Viruses[7]

Have you ever had a cold or the flu? The coughing and sneezing, aches and fevers are all the work of a tiny virus living inside some of your body's cells. How can such a tiny thing cause you to feel so awful? (_This paragraph does not have a main idea because it is an introduction to the rest of the piece._)

All living things, like plants and animals, share common behaviors that include growing, developing, reproducing, and responding to surroundings. Things that do not share these behaviors are nonliving things such as air, metal, and sand. Perched between the boundary of living and nonliving things are viruses, which are tiny, infectious particles that are considered by some scientists to be living things and by others to be nonliving things. If viruses are floating around in the air or sitting on a kitchen counter, they are inert, having as much life as a rock. However, unlike nonliving things, viruses can live and reproduce. When they attach to a suitable plant, animal, or bacterial cell, referred to as a host cell, they infect and take over the cell. To live and to reproduce, they must invade a host cell and use it. ⬦

Viruses are not cells, even though they have some substances also found in cells. Viruses are particles that are about a thousand times smaller than bacteria. These tiny particles contain genetic instructions that give the virus its characteristics, such as shape and how to reproduce. Viruses are wrapped in a protein coat. Some types of viruses also have a membrane around the protein. (_Implied main idea: "The structure of viruses"_) ▭

Divide this paragraph into two:

Viruses are around you all the time. They enter your body through your mouth or nose or through breaks in your skin. (_The first part of this paragraph does not support the rest of the paragraph, which is about viruses needing a certain type of host cell. This should be broken into two paragraphs_). ⬦

Different types of viruses require different types of host cells. The protein coat on the virus helps it detect the right kind of host cell. For example, a virus that causes a respiratory infection would detect and attack cells that line the lungs. ▽

Once the host cell is detected, the virus attaches itself to the outside of the cell (_adsorption_). It then injects its genetic information through the cell membrane and into the host cell (_entry_). The host cell's enzymes obey the virus's genetic instructions, creating new virus particles (_replication and assembly_). New particles leave the host cell in search of other host cells, where the cycle then continues

[7] Archer, A., Gleason, M., & Vachon, V. (2004). _REWARDS Plus: Reading strategies applied to science passages_ (Teacher's Guide, pp. 167–169). Longmont, CO: Sopris West Educational Services. Used with permission of the authors and publisher.

Exercise #7 (continued)

(_release_). The host cell may be destroyed during this process. As the virus spreads, you begin to feel more and more sick. Carefully examine the flowchart below to better understand how viruses work. (_Implied main idea: "How a virus spreads throughout a body"_) ▭

In order to look at a virus, you would have to look through an electron microscope. Electron microscopes are much more powerful than those you use at school, which may only be able to see bacteria. Remember that viruses are many times smaller than most bacteria cells. Scientists use electron microscopes to see the tiniest of particles. (_The main idea of this paragraph is spread over the last two sentences._) △

Different kinds of viruses have different shapes. Some viruses are polyhedral, meaning that they have many sides, while some are stick-shaped. Others look like they have pieces of string looped around them. One very common virus is shaped like a spaceship. ▽

Some basic steps can be taken to reduce the spread of viruses. People who have a cold or the flu should cover their mouths with a tissue when coughing or sneezing to help prevent others from getting the virus. They should also wash their hands before having contact with food or with other people. ▽

Divide this paragraph into two:

In addition, vaccines can be administered against some viruses. While a vaccine cannot cure a virus in someone who already has it, a vaccine can prevent a virus from infecting a person who doesn't have it yet. Vaccines teach the body how to produce proteins, called antibodies, which can intercept the virus in the bloodstream. An antibody acts like a key, which fits the keyhole on the virus and locks it up. (_The first part of this paragraph is about how vaccines work._) Some groups of people do not have antibodies against some diseases and other people do. Because they didn't have the matching antibodies, many of the first people who lived in the Americas in the 1600s were killed by viruses carried across the ocean by Europeans. In the current century, many people do have antibodies against the virus that causes AIDS, and thus they don't become ill even though they are infected. Yet, these infected people can still infect other people, some of whom might not have the antibodies. (_The main idea of this part of the paragraph is underlined_) ▽

An entirely new strain of a virus may appear even when a tiny change occurs in its genetic code, or instructions. The virus's genetic code can change rapidly, and it can significantly change the virus's shape. When the shape of the virus changes, the antibody key is no longer able to lock up the new virus. Because of this, vaccines often have to be updated frequently to prevent new waves of infection.

Our ability to see and understand viruses and bacteria has greatly increased in just the last twenty-five years. However, no matter what defenses we create, the genetic codes of viruses and bacteria are easily changed and create new problems for us to try to solve. (_This paragraph doesn't really have a main idea because it is a conclusion for the whole piece._) ▽

Exercise #8: Write Goldilocks Responses

◆ Read the following two paragraphs.

◆ Create a main idea for each paragraph that is too general, too specific, and just right for each paragraph.

Paragraph 1:

There was a war game that we little boys played after a big hunt. We went out a little way from the village and built some grass tepees, playing we were enemies and this was our village. We had an advisor, and when it got dark he would order us to go and steal some dried meat from the big people. He would hold a stick up to us and we had to bite off a piece of it. If we bit a big piece, we had to get a big piece of meat, and if we bit a little piece, we did not have to get so much. Then we started for the big people's village, crawling on our bellies, and when we got back without getting caught, we would have a big feast and a dance and make kill talks, telling of our brave deeds like warriors. Once, I remember, I had no brave deed to tell. I crawled up to a leaning tree beside a tepee and there was meat hanging on the limbs. I wanted a tongue I saw up there in the moonlight, so I climbed up. But just as I was about to reach it, the man in the tepee yelled "Ye-a-a!" He was saying this to his dog, who was stealing some meat too, but I thought the man had seen me, and I was so scared I fell out of the tree and ran away crying.

Too general: _Indian boys played games._

Too specific: _Indian boys tried to get meat from the big people's village._

Just right: _After a hunt, Indian boys played war games that tested their bravery and skill._

Paragraph 2:

Born in Italy in the middle of the 13th century, Marco Polo was part of a wealthy merchant family. His father and uncle had already been trading extensively with Middle Eastern countries. They traded silk, porcelain, and other exotic goods over the Silk Road. The Silk Road was a trading route established between China and Rome. As a result, the Polos traveled a great deal. Marco did not meet his father until he was 15 or 16, when his father returned to Venice after many years of travel. This time, when he left again, he took young Marco with him.

Too general: _Marco Polo's father took him traveling._

Too specific: _Marco didn't meet his father until he was 16._

Just right: _Because Marco Polo was born into a wealthy merchant family, he began traveling the world as a young man._

151

Exercise #9: Two-Column Notes About Mammals

◆ Reread the "What Is a Mammal?" passage on page 55–56.

◆ Complete the two-column notes that have been started (below) on the mammals passage. Note in the right column the important details for each subtopic listed in the left column.

Mammals	
First mammals on Earth	– 200 million years ago – evolved from extinct group of reptiles – were very small
Different types of mammals	– 4000 types of mammals – all have certain things in common
Three things in common	– warm-blooded vertebrates – have hair or fur – feed young with milk from mammary glands
Importance of hair and fur	– acts as insulation in cold climate
Mammals are warm-blooded	– can survive cold climate – internal temperatures stay the same
Circulatory system	– four-chambered heart and blood vessels – heart pumps blood to lungs to get oxygen – heart then pumps blood to all parts of the body
Excretory system	– kidneys filter waste from blood into urea – urea and water form urine – stored in bladder until passes out of body
Nervous system	– most highly developed brain – enables thinking and learning, coordinates movement, regulates body functions
Senses	– highly developed – some animals develop senses that are specific to survival in their physical environment

Exercise #9 (continued)

Reproduction	– internal fertilization – males and females are separate
Three types of reproduction	– egg-laying – pouched (grow in mother's pouch) – placental (born fully developed)

Exercise #10: Paraphrasing Subskills

◆ Each of these short activities builds the subskills that lead to more efficient and precise use of one's own words to take notes.

1. Substitute words for the underlined words:

   Hurricane Ivan caused a lot of damage when it passed through Mobile.

   Hurricane Ivan created havoc when it slammed into Mobile.

2. Mark nouns (**N**), verbs (**V**), adjectives (**adj**), and adverbs (**adv**):

   Brain studies consistently have shown that orthographic input stimulates medial extrastriate regions in the posterior left cerebral hemisphere.

   Brain (**adj**) studies (**N**) consistently (**adv**) have shown (**V**) that orthographic (**adj**) input (**N**) stimulates (**V**) medial (**adj**) extrastriate (**adj**) regions (**N**) in the posterior (**adj**) left (**adj**) cerebral (**adj**) hemisphere (**N**).

3. Find and circle the simple subject and the main verb in this sentence:

   Many of the colonies, rich in valuable natural resources, funneled wealth back into the British Empire.

   (Many) of the **colonies**, rich in valuable natural resources (funneled) wealth back into the British Empire.

4. Condense these three sentences into one sentence by combining the subjects and predicates:

   Marco was released from prison. The next year, he returned to Venice. He died there in 1324.

   After Marco was released from prison, he returned to Venice, where he died in 1324.

Exercise #11: Summarize!

◆ Write a one-paragraph summary of the RAND Heuristic on pages 8–12.

◆ Use the main ideas and details from the two-column notes you wrote in Exercise #1. Use the main ideas as the basis for your summary.

◆ Underline the transition words and phrases in your summary.

Comprehension is influenced by four variables: the reader, the text, the task, and the context for the task. The reader's background knowledge, ability to make inferences and construct mental images, and use of cognitive strategies affect comprehension. Second the complexity of text structure affects understanding. Another factor is the purpose of the reading task, including how extrinsic or intrinsic consequences affect the motivation to read. Finally, the amount of support and scaffolding available affects comprehension.

Exercise #12: Complete the Topic Web

- ◆ This is an incomplete topic web for Part III of this module (pages 39–83).

- ◆ Scan Part III in the Table of Contents to identify the missing topics.

- ◆ Fill in the blank flowchart.

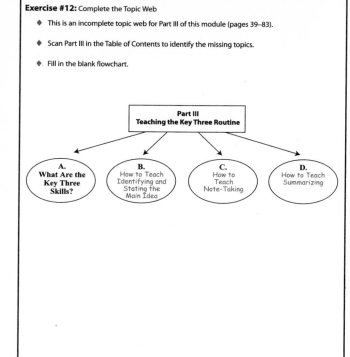

Exercise #13: Develop a Segment of a Topic Web Into a More Detailed Web

- ◆ The section topic "C. How to Teach Note-Taking" has been converted into the main heading of the web below.

- ◆ Skim the pages in this module about teaching note-taking (pages 68–77). Use the four bold-faced subheadings to complete the web.

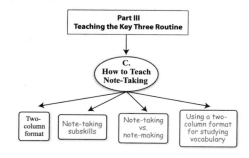

Exercise #14: Record Relevant Details

- ◆ Read the "Sherpas" passage and identify the paragraph main ideas.

- ◆ List the paragraph main ideas in the left column of the two-column note-taking template provided below.

- ◆ Then, record relevant details in paraphrases (your own words) in the right column, making a list rather than writing in complete sentences.

Sherpas

Paragraph Main Ideas	Relevant Details
Sherpas	– known as Mt. Everest climbing guides
	– have their own culture and customs
Yaks are important	– like a buffalo
	– fur and hide provide clothing and shoes
	– dung provides fuel and fertilizer
	– yak milk for food
Sherpas used to trade through the mountains with Tibet	– across Nangpa La Pass
	– herded yaks with items to trade
	– returned with salt and wool
	– trade has now stopped
Sherpa food	– grow potatoes
	– mix with meat and vegetables for stew
	– lentils and rice
	– drink tea

Exercise #14: Record Relevant Details (continued)

Paragraph Main Ideas	Relevant Details
Sherpa religious beliefs	– practice sect of Buddhism
	– honor mountains
	– believe Mt. Everest is home of goddess
	– used to keep mountains sacred by not climbing them
	– today they gather at Tengboche Monastery
Sherpa language	– difficult language related to modern Tibetan
	– two languages growing apart
	– Sherpa language not standardized
	– does not have written alphabet
Western climbers and Sherpas influence each other	– mountaineering became major industry by 1970s
	– Sherpas hired in cities as guides
	– Sherpas wear Western clothing
	– Sherpa culture has influenced climbers
Negative effects of mountaineering	– deforestation and litter
	– Everest base camp littered
	– recent efforts to clean up
Managing the forests and natural resources	– region declared a national park in 1976
	– Sherpa groups beginning to manage
	– will help to preserve culture and heritage

Exercise #15: Turning Topics Into Questions

♦ Using the notes you took in Exercise #14, turn the first four paragraph main ideas in the "Sherpas" passage into questions, and write them in the left column.

♦ Use the details to answer the questions in the right column.

Sherpas

Main idea questions	Details as answers
What are Sherpas known for?	- guiding expeditions up Mt. Everest - maintaining their own culture
Why are yaks important to Sherpas?	- yaks provide clothing, food, fuel, and fertilizer
How and what did Sherpas trade with their neighbors?	- drove yak herds across Nangpa La Pass to trade fur and clothing made from yaks for salt and wool
What do Sherpas grow and eat?	- potatoes and other vegetables - lentils, rice - tea

Exercise #16: Write a Summary From Main Idea and Detail Notes

♦ Using your main idea and detail notes on the "Sherpas" reading (Exercise #14), write a one-paragraph summary of the passage.

♦ Link your sentences with well-chosen transition words and phrases from Table 11.2 on page 80.

♦ Compare your summary with those of your colleagues.

Sample Summary

    Sherpas are mostly known as Mt. Everest climbing guides, but they have their own culture and customs. Yaks are an important part of Sherpa life because they are a source of clothing, fuel, fertilizer, and food. The Sherpas used to use their yaks to carry items to trade with Tibet through a mountain pass. The Sherpas grow most of their own food, such as potatoes. The Sherpas honor the mountains and believe they are sacred. The Sherpa language is related to Tibetan. However, it is more difficult to learn because it is not standardized and does not have a written alphabet. Western climbers and Sherpas have influenced each other in positive ways. Unfortunately, Western influence has also brought deforestation and litter to the mountains. Because the region was declared a national park, the forests are now being better managed.

Exercise #17: Schoolwide Implementation Checklist

♦ Using the guidelines stated above, check the steps or procedures that you need to undertake in your school or district in order to achieve schoolwide implementation of the Key Three Routine.

Participant answers will vary. Encourage discussion of results.